BE-ING @WORK

Heidi Forbes Öste, PhD

BE-ING @WORK

Wearables And Presence Of Mind In The Workplace

by
Heidi Forbes Öste, PhD

info@2BalanceU.com

Mill Valley, CA Boston, MA & Malmö, Sweden

Ordering Information:Quantity sales. Special discounts are available on quantity purchases by corporations, associations, and others. For details, contact the publisher at the address above.

Printed in the United States of America

BE-ING @WORK - First Edition 2017

ASIN: B074T36G64 (Amazon Kindle)

ISBN: 1977886019 (Createspace)

ISBN 13: 978-1977886019 (Createspace)

ISBN: 978-1-64136-773-8 (Ingram Spark) PAPERBACK

ISBN: 978-1-64136-772-1 (Ingram Spark) HARDCOVER

ISBN: 9781370687695 (Smashwords)

ASIN: B0721PP3KV

CONTACT THE AUTHOR:

2BalanceU.com

http://2BalanceU.com

info@2BalanceU.com

Mill Valley, CA Boston, MA & Malmö, Sweden.

Abstract

Expectations and demands in the changing contemporary workplace are driven by emergent technologies. Ubiquitous in nature, they are designed to enhance human and organization potential. These technologies provide access to information and connection at all times. They are increasingly reliant on human relationships and connection. BE-ing one's best self in each interaction amidst distraction and health-related issues challenge presence. Wellness and mindfulness in the contemporary workplace relate to individual health as well as productivity and engagement. The study examines the affordances of wearable technologies (wearables) in correlation to presence of mind in the workplace. Wellness wearables with functions related to potential causes of presenteeism (lost productivity from hindered presence) were used in this study. The findings are applicable for design, human resources and organization development professionals, and scholars. This study provides insight into potential interventions to meet the demands of the contemporary workplace through emerging technologies.

Key words: wearables, presence, presenteeism, productivity, sociomateriality, human computer interaction (HCI), social strategy, wearable technology, engagement, social technology, cognitive enhancement, workplace wellness, well-being, UX design

Acknowledgements

The path to this dissertation was both circuitous and often pulsing in pace. It was enriched by the contribution and support of many individuals along the way. Whether our paths crossed intentionally or by happenstance, my resulting work and I are the better for it. Numerous walk and talks, chats, Facebook messages, and video calls across the ocean gave me the strength and will to persevere. It is clear to me that I could not have done this alone.

There are a few people who I must thank specifically, beginning with my committee. Dorothy Agger-Gupta, thank you for introducing me to Fielding and being there throughout my journey as my champion and my chair. Jean-Pierre Isbouts, your feedback and encouragement kept me thinking about the big picture and striving for my best. Fred Steier, introducing me to sociomateriality removed my myopic blinders and made the final version shine. Kerry Mitchell, as my student reader, you provided so much more than fresh eyes on my writing when I could no longer discern the flow from the muck. My external examiner, Dr. Charlyn Belluzzo thank you for your inspiration to present and validate "soft" topics that have "hard" implications on organizations' well-being.

To Virgin Pulse, Interaxon, Jawbone, Misfit, OhMiBod, BlueTens, Samsung, and Lumo Body Tech, thank you for your generosity in providing devices and support to participants for my study. To each of my study participants thank you for being curious enough to participate.

A special thanks to my family and friends for your support during this, often tumultuous, journey. Mum, your undying confidence that I could do it helped me believe it too. My husband, Björn, and kids, Oskar and Hanna-Maria, I hope I have made you proud, despite many vacations interrupted. My girl posse, Caroline, Julie and Eliza, you are the best! My cohort, the Green Lanterns, you were with me every step of the way.

Table of Contents

CHAPTER ONE: INTRODUCTION TO THE STUDY 1

Introduction to the Study 1

Terminology 3

Motivation 5

Purpose 6

Significance 9

Conceptual Framework 10

Research Question 11

Limitations and Assumptions 12

Summary...13

CHAPTER TWO: REVEW OF THE LITERATURE..........................15

Design Thinking and Behavior...15

Presence in the Workplace 30

Social Technologies 45

Chapter 2 Summary..50

CHAPTER THREE: METHODOLOGY...51

Objective...51

Research Design..52

The Pilot 71

Data Analysis 71

Chapter 3 Summary 73

CHAPTER FOUR: FINDINGS 75

Participation 75

Quantitative Results from MAAS 76

Quantitative results for optimal presence 79

Findings from Qualitative Measures 82

Chapter 4 Summary 91

CHAPTER 5: DISCUSSION 93

Discussion 93

Implications 93

Limitations 104

Future Research 106

Conclusion 109

References 113

Can I Ask You For A Favor? 127

About The Author 129

CHAPTER ONE

INTRODUCTION TO THE STUDY

Introduction to the Study

The objective of this research was to explore the affordances of wellness wearable technology in correlation to the user's sense of presence in the contemporary workplace: being conscious and aware in the moment. Affordances refer to indirect effects of the wearables and the study. Wearables is a category of technological devices that can be worn by an individual that track and/or deliver data to the wearer. Presence was observed from two perspectives: sense of self and self with others. The intent of this study was to explore methods and cutting edge tools that can respond to the challenge of focus, distraction, and engagement in the workplace.

The contemporary workplace has many challenges that relate to health, wellness, and balance. Ubiquitous technologies provide both new opportunities and challenges to presence (Riva, Waterworth & Waterworth, 2004). The study focuses on presence in the workplace to explore the correlation to adoption of wearables. The potential is the ability to improve effectiveness and quality of interactions critical in a knowledge economy (Friedman & Friedman, 2015).

The relationship with technology designed to augment capabilities or even change behaviors relies on more than function (Fogg, 2003; Wendel, 2014). Design elements from purpose, form, function, delivery, support, infrastructure, maintenance, and ease of use affect technology's potential impact on presence, being in the moment. Access to immediate information and communication can be both helpful and a distraction (Lui & Wong, 2015; Rheingold & Weeks, 2012). The balance between enhancement and interruption is complex. This study explores both real and perceived affordances (Norman, 1999, 2009) of wearables in relation to presence. Design elements that impact one's ability to be present are part of the human-technical relationship explored.

Beyond profitability, the shift to purpose-driven strategies including people and planet is driving major changes in the workplace. From learning and development (Bingham & Conner, 2010, 2015) to leadership (George, Sims & Gergen, 2010; Li, 2010; Li & Solis, 2013) a deeper level of listening and higher sense of self-awareness is not only needed but also expected in contemporary human and organization systems. Return on relationships (Gummesson, 2004, Rubin, 2014) relies on presence to provide the value of the people to people connections. Social business strategies integrate social technologies into business and communications practices (Mishra & Evans, 2009: Kärkkäinen, Jussila & Väisänen, 2010). The new knowledge economy (Friedman & Friedman, 2015) presents both new opportunities but also challenges in a system based on trust in exchanges. Conscious business (Kofman, 2013) and social intelligence are considered the key success factors for the future (Goleman, 2006; Tan, Goleman & Kabat, 2014). They are critical components to understanding the human factors of business and leadership. Things get done because of people and the relationships between people.

This study focused on potential interventions to improve presence as it applies in the contemporary workplace. With improved presence comes the ability to improve quality of interactions, building of trust, and in turn engagement and productivity. This aspect of presence extends outside of the workplace into institutions and personal interactions. The study explored how the user perceives their presence and changes to their presence before, during, and after the use of wearables. The research is made available to the developers for the benefit of improving design and understanding potential opportunities for future development. The research also provides insight to organizations concerned about presenteeism (Hemp, 2004; DeBeer, 2014), mindlessness (Langer, 1985, 1989, 2009), and improving implementation of social strategy.

Terminology

For the purpose of this study the following operational definitions are used:

Affordances: The material properties of an environment (i.e., design of device, or study) that affects the way in which people interact with it and themselves.

Balance: A state in which elements are distributed in a manner that provides the greatest stability.

Balance Point: A state in optimal presence in which all of the states are equally present. At the optimal balance point, one has a sense of presence in which awareness of and engagement with self and other is achieved.

Devices: The different physical wearable technologies used for the purpose of the study.

Engagement: Employee commitment and passion that includes happiness, alignment, and job satisfaction.

Persuasive Design: Design with the intention of promoting behavioral change.

Intention: The conscious expression of purpose in an interaction usually based on personal and cultural values and/or experience, often misunderstood based on opposing intentions when either the sender or the receiver lacks mindfulness.

Materiality: The arrangement of an artifact's physical and/or digital materials into particular forms that endure across differences in place and time (Leonardi, 2013)

Mindfulness: Presence of mind in the moment without judgment.

Optimal Presence: When the contents of extended consciousness are aligned with the other layers of the self, and attention is directed towards a currently present external world (Waterworth & Riva, 2014).

Presence: Is a neuropsychological phenomenon; the non-mediated (pre-reflexive) perception of successfully transforming intentions in action within an external world (Riva, 2008).

Reciprocity: The evolutionary basis for cooperation in society (Nowak & Sigmund, 2000) as the giving of benefits to another in return for benefits received (Molm, 2010).

Presenteeism: A human resources concept referring to the situation when employees are physically present but presence of mind is hindered resulting in loss of productivity. The three subforms of presenteeism used in the context of this paper are health-related, disengagement, and cognitive.

Social Media Optimization: A marketing term used for managing content and media channels. This includes such concepts as search engine optimization (SEO) and use of content management systems that release content according to context in the best time slots and channels to reach a target audience.

Social Optimization: A social strategy term describing a method for optimizing relationships in both online and offline context. It is used to describe the methods and mindset required for building and maintaining mutually beneficial and effective relationships using social tools from events to social networks and applications (Forbes Öste, 2009, 2013).

Social Strategy: Strategic application of the philosophy of social business, in which social technologies supported by new approaches facilitate a more open, engaged, and collaborative foundation for how we work (Li & Solis, 2013)

Social Technologies: Digital technology that enables interaction between people: smart phones, social media, wearable tech, tablets, social gaming, augmented reality, music sharing, social shopping, social search, location-based services, and so forth.

Sociomateriality: An emerging concept referring to the fusion of social (institutions, norms, discourses, and all other social phenomena) and material (technology and other objects) (Orlikowski & Scott, 2008; Leonardi, 2013; Mutch, 2013; Parmiggiani & Mikalsen, 2013)

Wearables: Electronic devices that are worn on the body, often embedded into clothing or accessories. They integrate the use of sensors and/or communications capability for connection to other devices and data.

Wellness: A state of complete physical, mental, and social well-being, and not merely the absence of disease or infirmity (World Health Organization, 1948).

Wellness Wearables: A category of wearable technology that is used for devices with the function related to health and/or wellness.

Workplace: Physical location where someone works. In the contemporary workplace this can be a remote home office, a café, in a large office, or any combination or variation.

Motivation

In early 2014, listening to a conference panel share their stories about wearable tech and hardwiring the brain, it was like a light bulb went off. I began my doctoral journey determined to explore the theoretical underpinnings of social strategy consulting: teaching effective integration of emerging social technologies into organization culture and practice. The elusive missing piece was the self-awareness and presence required to engage authentically and productively. The skills for adopting new social technologies in the contemporary workplace require more than technical training. Without self-awareness or presence of mind, their efforts in engagement can result in distrust and miscommunication that goes viral. It is putting the theory into practice and behavior change that is the challenge. Hardwiring the brain for greater self-awareness and presence with self and others seemed like a good place to start.

I stayed to listen to several more panels on wearable technologies. Each one of them made my heart race as I thought of the possibilities. They spoke of wearables designed to train focus, posture, sleep, activity, and wellness. I thought of my own challenges to presence and realized that each of these were common in the workplace. At the time, I was using the fitness band, Jawbone UP®, to motivate training after knee surgery. I noticed a remarkable difference in my mood and focus simply from increasing my daily movement and awareness of my diet. The connection between physiological and psychological was profound in the experience. These emerging technologies, wearables, potential to trigger a shift in presence and productivity struck me as worthy of further investigation.

Purpose

Human Resources, also known as People Departments, are shifting their attention from recruitment and incentive programs (hiring and retaining) to including a more holistic people-centered focus. The top 2015 industry priorities include increasing engagement, retention, and employee wellbeing (Turgis, Allen & Xiao, 2015). A wave of wellness programs that include mindfulness, exercise, and happiness is sweeping global organizations. If Google's Search Inside Yourself Leadership Institute (SIYLI), Zappos' Tony Hseih's Delivering Happiness, General Mills' Institute for Mindful Leadership, and Jeff Weiner of LinkedIn's Conscious Leadership are any indication, we are looking at a big shift toward transformation. These movements focus on the positive effects in flow, productivity, collaboration, innovation, culture, social intelligence, and general happiness on their organizations. Their examples are inspiring others to follow the wave.

One indication of the need for this shift is impaired productivity due to presenteeism (Hemp, 2004). De Beer (2014) extends Presenteeism beyond loss of productivity due to health impairment (health-related presenteeism) to include motivational aspects like boredom, challenge, or distraction (disengagement presenteeism). Numerous studies reveal the cost of presenteeism to be at least 1.5 times higher than that of absenteeism (Goetzel et al., 2004; Cooper & Dewe, 2008). Physical presence at work, without presence of mind can result in not only impaired productivity, but also potentially greater incidence of miscommunication and distrust.

I suggest that presenteeism has far higher numbers in the contemporary workplace. Some of the elements are inter-related to their psychological or physiological counterparts. The average smart phone users check their phone 150 times a day (Meeker & Wu, 2013). Increasingly, there is need for treatment of stress and anxiety from fear of missing out (FoMO; Bragazzi & Del Puente, 2014), and mobile phone addiction (nomophobia; Archer, 2013). These intersect with both health-related and disengagement presenteeism. That is not to discount the recognized challenges related to health and productivity in the modern workplace as a result of stress, poor diet, sedentary lifestyle, depression, and back strain (Ratey, 2008, De Beer).

Buck Consultants produce a report on "Working Well: A Global Survey of Health Promotion and Workplace Wellness" annually, exploring emerging trends in health and wellness programs provided by employers. Most notable was the addition in 2014 of productivity to the scope in recognition of employers increased emphasis on the connection between wellbeing and performance. In the 2009 and 2012 studies, health-related presenteeism ranked number one almost across the board. If taken in the wider context used to include disengagement and cognitive presenteeism (which I will elaborate on later), the top two priorities would remain presenteeism and employee engagement almost across the globe. Presenteeism and employee engagement are still top priorities in the majority of countries.

Table 1

Extent to which certain health risks and issues drive wellness strategy by region (Buck Consultants, 2014). Reproduced with permission.

	All regions*	Africa/ Middle East	Asia	Australia/ NZ	Canada	Europe	Latin America	United States
Stress	1	2	4	2	1	1	2	3
Physical activity/exercise	2	5	2	1	2	2	4	1
Nutrition/healthy eating	3	8	6	3	3	3	5	2
Workplace safety	4	1	1	5	9	6	1	12
Work/life issues	5	2	13	4	6	4	8	9
Depression/anxiety	6	8	11	8	5	5	7	10

1 = highest impact, 17 = lowest impact

Ranked 1st   Ranked 2nd   Ranked 3rd

Many different standards for measurement exist to ascertain the impact; the costs of lost productivity and engagement are hard to establish and debated (Cancelliere, Cassidy, Ammendolia & Côté, 2011). Sleep disturbances cause fatigue-related productivity losses estimated at $1,967 per employee annually (Rosekind, Gregory, Mallis, Brandt, Seal & Lerner, 2010). The cost of depression in the US worker-related productivity losses cost nearly $2 billion (Birnbaum, Kessler, Kelley, Ben-Hamadi, Joish & Greenberg, 2010). The complex nature of ascertaining the root causes of lost productivity represents the complexity of humans and the systems in which they and their organizations operate and perform. Successful interventions for presenteeism have a potential high return on investment.

Our relationship with technology is also complex. How technology is integrated into our lives can vary from casual use to dependence. In Turkle's (2011) work around being alone together, she describes a world where we are immersed in our devices. According to Turkle, in order to combat addiction, you have to discard the addicting substance. Technology is here to stay. We therefore need to seek new paths to connect. Many parents of teenagers today observe this obsession first hand (and perhaps are guilty of it themselves). Nomophobia, the fear of being without your mobile phone, afflicts 40% of the population (Archer, 2013) of 58% of the adult population that have mobile phones. Due to its increase in prevalence, Bragazzi and Del Puente (2014) proposed including nomophobia in the Diagnostic and Statistical Manual of Mental Disorders (DSM).

The "why" may vary as to the cause for lack of presence. What is clear is that there is a problem. Distraction and disengagement affect productivity, innovation, culture of organizations, and human relationships. These are critical in the social era (Merchant, 2012) where connection, purpose, and community are key to people and organization's ability to thrive. It is important to seek new ways to overcome this challenge. For some it may be through mindfulness practices, and building self-awareness. For others it may be treating an affliction that is leading to lack of presence. This may display in chronic pain, device addiction, disrupted flow, social disconnect, poor mental or physical health. Now let's look at the "how" to fix it.

Significance

The opportunities for wearable technologies to solve existing problems and challenges are exciting. So exciting, that many are vying for a piece of this emerging market estimated to be worth over $12B by 2018 (ABI Research, 2013), more recently estimated at $37B by 2020 (TechSci Research, 2015). This figure elicits both buzz and skepticism. If the representation of wearable technologies from smart watches and glasses, medical devices, and fitness trackers to fashion are any sign, the prediction may be accurate and even a conservative estimate. Limited study beyond functional capacity in relation to the workplace has been conducted thus far, despite their appearance in the workplace via both user initiative as well as company wellness programs.

Despite the excitement, design challenges both in form and function hinder the category's mainstream adoption. Experts echo that strapping a smart phone to your wrist is NOT wearable technology. "Wearable tech must be wearable," as Misfit Wearables founder, Sonny Vu says (2014, personal communication). Early mobile phones had similar challenges related to design, signal strength, battery size, price, supporting infrastructure (Mobile 50, 2007). All of these elements continue to evolve closer to achieving critical mass for mass-market usage and connection. Wearables are still in their relative infancy. These factors need to be taken into consideration in this study. This study is a significant step towards providing insight into development of future wearables solutions and their potential application in the workplace.

As the technology improves in accuracy, power, durability, usability, and wearability, and the interfaces become more integrated, the value beyond novelty will be clearer. We see this already in the advances in fitness wearables. They are making a dent in one of the most profound issues of today: getting people out of their seats and moving (Owen, Healy, Matthews & Dunstan, 2010). This research will provide some answers to the burning question of outcomes being asked in the greater communities from wellness providers to wearable developers to human relations managers.

Conceptual Framework

The conceptual framework of this study includes elements from design and behavior, presence in the workplace, and social strategy. These three elements overlap as they apply to the emerging technologies and the demands of the contemporary workplace. As will be shown in the literature review in Chapter 2, the tools sometimes cause the change, but can also be the solution.

Design and Behavior. The design of wearable technology involves elements beyond the physical device. Designing for behavior change involves understanding psychology, behavioral economics, design, and of human computer interaction. Each of these elements were explored further as applied to wearables and presence of mind in the workplace.

Presence in the Workplace. Presence-of-mind in the workplace extends beyond the physical and relates to the awareness and attention to the moment. This is explored more extensively as it applies to the ability to be productive and engaged, particularly in the contemporary workplace. The demand for an application of and means for presence apply to many layers of organizations from the individual to the system in which they operate.

Social Technologies. In the contemporary workplace, disruptive digital technologies like social media, video conferencing, and smart phones changed the way individuals and organizations communicate. Unintended consequences of miscommunication or communication lacking awareness of self and/or the audience have magnified impact. Much of the literature in this area is practice based, yet no less applicable. The implications on behavior, leadership, relationships, and communication, not to mention design of the tools that enable the interactions intersect with both design and presence. Wearables and their accompanying apps are social tools. The use (or not) and the policies (or lack thereof) that drive social tool use in organizations are critical to the development of successful social strategy. In the context of this study, wearables use was examined in correlation to self-awareness with the intent to improve quality of interactions, and diminish the frequency of failed interactions that go viral.

Research Question

Are there affordances from wellness wearable technologies that correlate with sense of presence-of-mind in the workplace?

Secondary questions and exploration into the following:

- What are the potential design and user challenges when adopting wearable technologies for undesirable behaviors modification or health-related impairments?
- What is the potential impact of wearables use on presenteeism and mindlessness in the workplace?
- Is there a correlation between wearables technologies and quality of social interactions, related to self-assessed sense of presence with others?
- Is there a correlation between increased awareness of self from the physiological to the psychosocial (through wearable data and experience).

Limitations and Assumptions

The rapid advances in the field of wearable technology limit the ability to do a study that captures the most recent development. This study attempted to integrate new updates as they came readily available. As mentioned previously, wearables are still in their relative infancy; these factors were taken into consideration in this study. As such, there is an assumption that issues may arise related to early release rather than the potential of a mature product tested over time.

Inquiry into one's sense of presence weekly may influence one's awareness of his or her sense of presence. This was not avoidable without misleading the participants as to the purpose of the study. That said, the influence provided additional data worth capturing as potential alternate interventions outside of, or with, wearables. This was taken into consideration in both the analysis and design of the study.

As to assumptions, there was a certain level of tech savvy or comfort expected with the participants simply in the requirement of a smartphone to use the wearables. Although the penetration of smartphone usage on U.S. adults is somewhere between 64%

and 72% depending on whose data you use (Pew Research Center, 2015: Nielson, 2014) and in many countries it is far less. The ability to generalize in this context is limited to digital citizens (Schein, 2014).

Summary

Changing dynamics and requirements of the contemporary workplace call for greater social intelligence (Goleman, 2006): self-awareness and empathy, presence. New technologies are both a hindrance to our abilities as well as an opportunity to augment or improve them. Although in their infancy, the emerging category of wearable technology (wearables) may provide some solutions. This study explored the potential correlation between wellness wearables use with sense of presence in the workplace. The implications and limitations of current wearables were also considered. The intent was to understand how best to apply emerging technologies in the workplace for greater benefit to individuals, the organizations in which they work, and the systems in which they engage. We will now look at the literature in design, presence, and social technologies to explore what is behind each of the elements.

CHAPTER TWO

REVEW OF THE LITERATURE

Design Thinking and Behavior

(Unintended or unforeseen) affordances are identified and capitalized upon. When developing a new category such as wearables, this type of feedback is critical in the development process. Intended outcomes may be far from the goal, but may achieve an alternate beneficial outcome not identified at the outset.

To make sense of the world, we're always trying to place things in context, whether our environment is physical, cultural, or something else altogether. Now that we live among digital, always-networked products, apps, and places, context is more complicated than ever—starting with "where" and "who" we are (Hinton, 2015, p.2)

Human behavior is complex and responds based on both nature and nurture. Equally complex are the ways in which we organize, process and react to information and physical stimuli of our environments. The use of information architecture and design thinking as tools to provide clarity in the complexity is increasingly important. Designing new products and services require a deeper understanding of the context of the users based on how they perceive and understand their environments, context (Gibson, 1979): relationships.

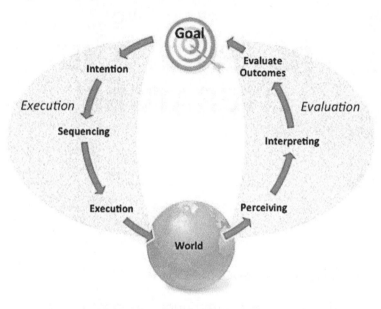

Figure 1. Model for design for action (Norman, 2013).
Adapted with permission.

Norman (1988, 2013) expanded upon Gibson's (1979, 2015) work to extend beyond relationships to perceived affordances that result in action. Developers and designers in the field of human computer interaction (HCI) apply Norman's model for understanding the cycle of action (Figure 1) as it relates to design from concept development, execution, and evaluation for further iterations. Norman's model relates the importance of the cycles that involve dividing the execution stages (design for action process) as well as evaluation (iteration process) into a repeating cycle. This creates a system accounting for affordances in the design process. The goal and world/system are the constants. That said, when the goal is change, the model still applies but is more malleable at either end as the conditions may change (thus the cycle continues). Nonetheless, establishing the intention of the action and planning for the sequence and execution of action are necessary steps that lead to launch (connection with the world/system). The evaluation begins with understanding the outcomes in perception then interpretation of the perception and evaluation of the interpretation before revising or determining if the goal (or a different outcome) is achieved.

The current pace of new version/product releases requires methods that enable rapid development and launch with feedback and evaluation embedded. This is demonstrated in the "Ship-it" approach to product release (Richardson & Gewaltney, 2005). Using ship-it, many products are released in extended beta versions allowing for users to be involved in the development and iteration process. Within this approach, both perceived and hidden (unintended or unforeseen) affordances are identified and capitalized upon. When developing a new category such as wearables, this type of feedback is critical in the development process. Intended outcomes may be far from the goal, but may achieve an alternate beneficial outcome not identified at the outset.

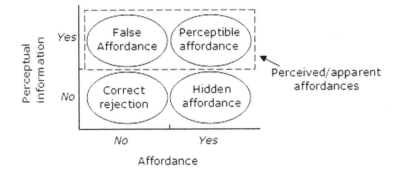

Figure 2. Hidden affordance (Gaver, 1996).
Used with permission.

Hidden affordances (Figure 2) of wearables are of great value to designers to explore. Gaver (1996) applied ecological psychology (study of perception and action) to social interaction as it relates to affordances. Gaver refers to the affordances of paper, as opposed to electronic mail, in relation to response time and expectation of content. Given the rise in use of short message services (SMS) or text, this could be further evaluated to explore the affordances of the changing medium.

I would extend his approach to include the context of this work, wearables. How one is perceived or how one believes he or she is perceived by another, while wearing a physically visible camera such as Google Glass, might influence the behavior of both individuals as well as the intended effect of the device itself. Additionally, consider texts produced through dictation software interpreting voice: an expedient but often inaccurate tool with non-retrievable output. Design as it evolves today must take into account the social interaction affordances, in particular the hidden affordances that are more challenging to identify.

Wurman described the emerging field of Information Architecture as focusing upon clarity, human understanding, and the organization of information (Wurman, 1996; Hinton, 2015). The explosion of information and knowledge easily accessible via the Internet resulted in a need for navigation and organizational tools and expertise. The democratization and globalization of information creates an added level of complexity (Ding & Lin, 2009). Since exacerbated by the proliferation of smartphones and the growing Internet of Things (IoT), the need for structured information in order to simplify navigation is a moving target that continues to rapidly evolve. The principles of information architecture are critical in the design process, particularly when the intent is to influence behavior.

Applying the principles of information architecture: planning, research, structural design (defining the ontology, taxonomy, and choreography), defines how physical information is processed and action taken by the users. These efforts in the early development process increase the chances of success in new products and services, as well as improvement or change of existing ones.

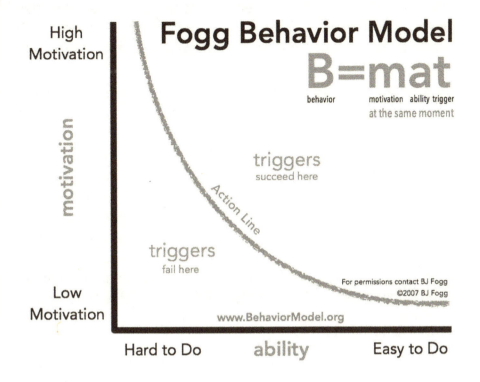

Figure 3. Fogg behavior model for persuasive design (Fogg, 2007). Used with permission.

In design, these principles are critical from planning to development and implementation or launch of complex devices and services that seamlessly integrate into an already complex world. B.J. Fogg of the Stanford Design Center created a model for persuasive design (2007) that is widely used today (see figure 3).

In Fogg's behavior model, the three elements (motivation, ability, and trigger) simultaneously result in a desired behavior. The sports team Golden State Warriors applied Fogg's model in a campaign to increase conversion rates at concessions. Using a fan application (app) on a smart phone in the stadium notified (trigger) the user about a deal (motivation) at the concession stand as one is walked by (ability) it. One might further enable the behavior by a direct pay feature (ability) directly through near field communication (NFC) technology from a wearable, further removing the barriers to action.

The device functionality is part of a process flow, but does not cause the change in isolation: Behavior = motivation + ability + trigger (B=mat). Understanding their users' behavior and motivators, and the triggers needed to create an action are part of the persuasive design being used in the development of many new products and services today.

Wendel's action funnel model (figure 4; 2014) further extends Fogg's work (2003, 2007, 2012) to assert the preconditions for action: cue, reaction, evaluation, ability, timing, and execute (CREATE) must exist. Wendel suggests that some of these can be automated through defaults to improve chances of success. In behavior change, understanding the user is paramount. For the model to be effective, designers need to understand the user's experience and the value ascribed to the product and action by the user.

Applying the model to wearables, an example might be that a user does not share the designer's vision for improving healthcare through compiling meta-data from all devices. The user's interest in sharing his or her data is limited to his/her personal benefit in tracking his/her weight loss until their goal is achieved. Movement may increase, but the misalignment does not meet the goal of the product for the company.

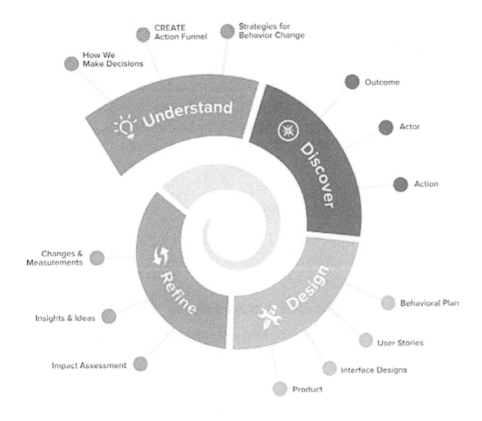

Figure 4. Wendel's action funnel model for designing for behavior change (Wendel, 2014). Reproduced with permission.

Interaction design incorporates design and behavior principles based on research. Moggridge (2007) explains the challenge of innovative design and developing prototypes for people in new categories. "If your goal is innovative design, your product or service has not even been thought of, so by definition it cannot be explained to research" (p.664). This paradox is presented in Norman's more recent work the Design of Future Things. Both describe, if not directly allude to, the importance of social intelligence and the understanding of the human factors as well as the changing landscape when developing new products and services. Things are not just things, but they are connected. They must interact and fit with people's increasingly complex lives creating a perceived value beyond the new and shiny.

When it comes to the design of wearables, the element of "wearability" gets much attention. In this context a report by Motti and Caine (2014) sheds some light on the human-centered principles pertaining to designing for wearability as they apply to wearable technology. The 20 factors identified are as follows:

1. Aesthetics
2. Affordance (by their definition, intuitive interaction)
3. Comfort
4. Contextual awareness
5. Customization (look and feel)
6. Ease of use (simple intuitive interface)
7. Ergonomy (physical shape with regard to body anatomy)
8. Fashion
9. Intuitiveness
10. Obtrusiveness (i.e., physiological sensors and how they interact with the body)
11. Overload (human cognitive limitations)
12. Privacy (both interaction and with respect to collected data)
13. Reliability (safety, precision, and effectiveness)
14. Resistance (abrasion, impact, temperature, humidity, flexure, laundering, durability)
15. Responsiveness (limited disruption to user's productivity)
16. Satisfaction (emotionally and functionally)
17. Simplicity
18. Subtlety
19. User friendliness

20. Wearability (dynamic wearability referring to a body in motion)

Wearability is only one of many factors that affect the user experience. Rowland, Goodman, Charlier, Light and Lui (2015) take many of these human factors into account from the user experience design (UX) perspective when designing connected products. Interoperability, interactions that span multiple devices, define whether devices and apps integrate into existing tech ecosystems. For example, platform-specific applications for controlling connected devices limit wider user base (i.e., Apple iOS, Android, or Windows). Service design looks at the lifespan of the customer experience (device interactions, customer support, instructions, software updates, marketing materials). The conceptual model ensures the users' expectations are met. Users are prepared to use the device correctly and can grow to understand its full capabilities through use.

Productization is the value proposition that creates a market or fulfills an existing need. The platform design creates an environment in which to manage devices and data as well as add new ones. Each of these pieces in isolation will not ensure successful user experience design (UX design). The holistic approach of UX design, especially in products that are so intimately related to the human experience is apparent in the rising demand for UX design expertise in organizations (Dishman, 2015). Wearables aside, the rise in smart phone applications to service consumers requires many of the same design factors.

Wearables. There is no denying the integration of technology in our lives, the ubiquitous nature of devices and their use. With it, sociomateriality (Orlikowski & Scott, 2008: Leonardi, 2013: Parmiggiani & Mikalsen, 2013: Mutch, 2013: Gaskin, Berente, Lyytinen & Yoo, 2014) has emerged as an ontological lens exploring the mutually constitutive and developing relationship between humans and technologies. With sociomateriality, they co-exist creating meaning from one another. As Brian Solis (2015) states, "experiences are products" rather than the counter. Whether wearable or simply part of our daily routines of interaction, the interdependence is profound.

Devices in the Market. The wearable category is still relatively new. Similar to early mobile phones, their potential was not fully exploited until the design, technology, and infrastructure caught up with the innovation. We now can fit a mobile phone with the computing power and functionality exceeding computers of that time in our pockets. Wearables have the same challenges, but advances that make them smaller, more energy efficient, and less disruptive to our routines are in development.

Devices continue to improve as issues with sensor accuracy, battery life, and communication between device and smartphones advance. Figure 5 illustrates the trade-offs in accuracy that wearable developers face.

Figure 5: Accuracy trade-offs in wearable devices (Inside

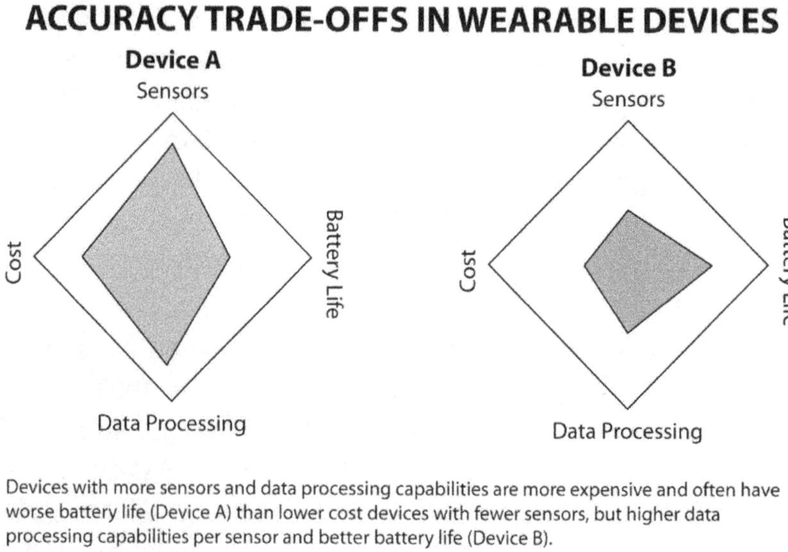
ACCURACY TRADE-OFFS IN WEARABLE DEVICES
Device A
Sensors
Cost
Battery Life
Data Processing
Device B
Sensors
Cost
Battery Life
Data Processing
Devices with more sensors and data processing capabilities are more expensive and often have worse battery life (Device A) than lower cost devices with fewer sensors, but higher data processing capabilities per sensor and better battery life (Device B).

Activity Tracking). Reproduced with Permission

These limitations, coupled with the expectations, are amongst the greatest challenges for mainstreaming wearable technology. Expectations of the devices' accuracy and frustrations with battery life come at the cost of accuracy. The cost per device rises with improved and increased sensors and increased battery life (while limiting the size). This makes them inaccessible to a large part of the market. As the prices come down and the sensors improve, there should be a shift in users much like the adoption of the smartphone.

Wearable device design is subject to the limited pace of innovation in energy, sensors, connection, and interfaces as well as infrastructure and operating systems and the requirements for compliance. Developments in the near future in solar, kinetic, and other ambient energy harnessing as well as sensors and communication will create a whole new wave in integrative design. The technology will continue to evolve and become further embedded in users' lives through fabrics and formats that feel less invasive and disruptive.

Devices in Lifestyle. Concerns over intrusiveness of wearables as they become increasingly embedded in our lives still carry a great deal of voice (Thierer, 2014). The ubiquitous nature of the smart phone and wearables naturally presents a shift. What was previously the water cooler conversation is now often delivered through a text, Tweet, YouTube Video, or Snapchat. Conversations now have greater resonance both in distance and volume.

When Bluetooth headsets first hit consumers, they seemed like something out of science fiction. Headsets are now standard accessories for mobile phones in compliance with hands-free safety requirements. Their functionality was needed to lift eyes away from the screen, particularly when operating vehicles. Nonetheless, the nonverbal message of wearing a headset when interacting with another individual face to face is either the wearer is actively on a call or anticipating one, therefore not fully present.

Devices that capture more than text, particularly photo or video, have increased concerns over privacy. They also provide incredible opportunity for productivity in applied ecosystems such as surgical and logistics. Wearers of Google Glass, smart eyewear with an optical head-mounted display (OHMD), were referred to as "glassholes." Some locations forbid their use in certain public settings. Of course it is hard to have "what happens in Vegas, stay in Vegas" when actions are being captured and shared through social media. Security of information and developments can be put at risk. From a behavioral standpoint, real or perceived, invasions of privacy change the way people behave in everyday life. On a positive note, the placement of the screen has the ability to keep the user's eyes raised and posture upright, instead of staring down at a screen in his or her hands.

The 2015 Consumer Electronics Show (CES) in Las Vegas, a mecca for all things new and innovative (and geeky), displayed an enormous rise in the representation of wearable devices. Some of the devices accompany smartphones to extend their functionality (few were an attempt to miniaturize the smartphone itself). The sensor-based health and fitness category had a decent representation, although still dominated by several players.

Gender-specific devices are becoming more prevalent, both in styling and function. The goal is to make wearables more wearable. Smartwatches are still somewhat the domain of men, being large and somewhat unattractive. The recently launched AppleWatch™ targeted this issue with its variable styling and size. Although critics argue it is still too big and should not require the iPhone™ for connection, its sales reflect success in overcoming gender barriers.

Investors are racing to invest in wearables able to overcome the design challenge. Disguised as jewelry, designers are creating devices that users will wear even when not functioning. Ringly™, a ring that provides light and vibration notifications of critical incoming calls, texts (whatever is assigned to it) received $50 million in funding to expand its line. Women who miss calls while the phone is in a purse are clambering for the device. Cuff™, a bracelet that both sends and receive notifications, enabling the user to send out an alert for help to friends and family, received $5 million. Both Ringly™ and Cuff™

are targeted to women both in their form and functionality. Misfit's partnership with Swarovski™ crystals for a solar-powered Shine™, fitness and sleep tracker, is also in this category.

Integration of sensors and displays into clothing is on the rise. Mostly somewhat novel, and highly priced, the potential is enough that many designers are collaborating with developers to experiment and identify opportunities. The sportswear category already has traction. OMsignal™ biometric smartwear reads biometrics and shares them via an app with the user and loved ones or healthcare providers. Sensoria™ socks measure cadence and foot landing. These two weave the technology into the fabrics. Misfit and other fitness tracking manufacturers are designing clothing and jewelry that integrate placement for their devices.

Devices at Work. Corporate wellness programs are rapidly adopting fitness trackers and wellness wearables as a way to collect health data and incentivize increased activity. In the US, this has been spurred by preventative care incentives provided established in the Affordable Care Act. The recurrent dialog at the July 2014 Digital Health Summit was on incentives for use of wearable devices for tracking patients' health. This includes sharing the data with their primary healthcare provider.

The other ongoing questions were regarding outcomes of use beyond functionality and how to keep people using the devices long enough for the outcomes to surface and sustain. Incentive programs provide discounted coverage for fitness wearables use and participation in health tracking. Another approach using gamification, competitive social games with intended outcome or output like weight loss or activity, has encouraged continued use of the devices.

The shift in health care models integrating wearables also means reimbursement for the devices is most likely soon to come to fruition. As of now, most fitness wearables are only Federal Trade Commission (FTC) compliant. In January 2015, the Food and Drug Administration (FDA) discussed the requirement of validation on health claims for wearable devices. The initial draft, as of 20 January identifies that wearables will not be considered medical devices unless they make claims about fitness to treat specific diseases or conditions, or present inherent risks to consumers' safety (2015). Among claims allowed are those related to weight management, physical fitness, mental acuity, self-esteem, sleep management, relaxation or stress management, or sexual function.

In other words, it is okay to say it helps you focus, but not to claim that it works for attention deficit disorder (ADD) without the application and extensive clinical trials required for FDA approval. For the purpose of this study, I will be using non-medical-grade wearable devices that fit in the wellness, fitness, and notifications categories.

Some organizations embrace the opportunity for employees to choose devices that are based on individuals' needs, styles, and interests. Others have specified devices that they support through Bring-your-own-device (BYOD) policies. The policies, not unlike those created for social media use, often require input from legal, technical, public relations, and communications.

Mindful device use has potential to provide considerable enhancement or augmentation. But self-awareness is required for this to take place. It has been shown that doing two relatively complex tasks simultaneously deteriorates performance measurably (Norman, 2013). With continual situation awareness, interruptions like notifications similarly disrupt performance. This will be taken into consideration in the qualitative interview segment of the study.

The Research. In the last 2 years there have been two notable studies looking into the wearables and the potential to impact behavior in the workplace. In particular they looked at the effect on productivity. Both Wilson (2013) and the Rackspace (Rackspace & Goldsmiths, 2014) studies have been heavily referred to given the dearth of scholarly research on wearables in the workplace, to date.

Wilson (2013) presented the concept of Physiolytics, "the practice of linking wearable computing devices with data analysis and quantified feedback to improve performance." Physiolytics, according to Wilson, provides three kinds of analysis. The first is quantification of movements within physical work environments. Second, the ability to work with information more efficiently relates to the ergonomics of the device's information delivery. The third form of analysis is the quantification of physiological functions (the capture of big data). Big data is that which is captured and quantified by the devices, then delivered in some spreadsheet or app format.

The study was performed in a Tesco warehouse tracking workers' movement, task completion, and timing. Wilson's study focused on the physiological aspects of wearables, but suggests that these are indicators of potential for use in both improved health and cognitive performance. His term was picked up by the quantified-self movement of athletes trying to understand and track their physical data for performance improvements. It is worth noting that in the 2 years since his article was released the capabilities of the sensors have already evolved greatly.

The Human Cloud at Work, a collaborative project ending in 2014 between Dr. Chris Brauer of Goldsmiths, University of London, and Rackspace, a cloud-based data storage company, studied the impact of wearable technologies on the workplace. The findings were positive toward the ability of wearables to improve productivity. The study also identified potential information technology (IT) challenges specifically in managing the data. The third finding was that participants were less concerned with the big brother aspect of sharing their data than was anticipated.

The Rackspace wearables study identified the potential for the increasing role they will play in productivity and job satisfaction. Their results showed 8.5% increased productivity and 3.5% increase in job satisfaction. The devices used in the study were brainwave monitoring Neurosky Mindwave™ and LumoBack™ for posture. The focus on the study was productivity and performance. Brauer (Rackspace & Goldsmith, 2014) notes the results are in line with the

"Hawthorne effect" of enhanced performance due to the fact that their performance is being monitored even when self-monitored.

Presence in the Workplace

In recent years interest and demand for greater presence has increased. What presence actually means has a wide range of applications and schools for debate. At its most basic level there is a greater need for awareness and engagement with the here and now. "Here" becomes less clear as we move from face-to-face to virtual to blended interactions. "Now" even loses clarity with global interactions that often include a-synchronous elements blended with the synchronous. The ability to "be" in both "here" and "now" requires a high level of self and other awareness and engagement that varies depending on the situation. This critique explores the definitions and applications of presence that are driving this interest and demand in organizations.

What is Presence? Presence as a construct resides in many forms: time, being, place, existence, and impression of (real, imaginary, or virtual). Scholars and practitioners in philosophy from Artistotle to Heidegger have long discussed presence. More currently it is used in psychology (Brown & Ryan, 2003; Langer, 1989; Morgan & Morgan, 2005), medicine (De Beer, 2014; Kabat-Zinn, 2007), neuroscience (Beeli, Casutt, Baumgartner, & Janke, 2008; Ratey, 2008; Siegel, 2007), leadership and organizations (Hewlett, Leader-Chivee, Sherbin, Gordon, & Dieudonne, 2014;, Kahn, 1992; Reid, 2009; Scharmer, 2000; Senge, Scharmer, Jaworski, & Flowers, 2005), theology (Dalai Lama, 2008), and technology (Waterworth & Riva, 2014). This dissertation will focus on the significant recent contributions relating to the evolving definition and expectations of presence as outlined earlier.

How the construct of presence is applied in each has evolved with the discussion and players at hand. Heidegger (1889-1976) used Anwesenheit (presence) and vorhanden (present-at-hand), truth and dasein (being), and ontology. Aristotle's nun (now-moment) is more temporal in nature, and expresses its opposing characteristic of "absence." Psychologists provide the reflective mind of attention and awareness where the mind is present (being) in the moment (temporal). The construct built upon by later scholars extends beyond the state and condition into how it affects both the self other to include action-based elements of "doing."

The works of De Beer (2014), Morgan and Morgan (2005), Brown and Ryan (2003), Langer (1989, 2009, 2014), Reid (2008, 2009), Riva, Waterworth, & Waterworth (2004), Waterworth and Riva (2014), Riva (2008) and Scharmer (2000) are examined in the context of optimal presence in today's human and organization systems. The term optimal presence is used both by Morgan and Morgan, in psychotherapy, as well as by Waterworth and Riva, in human-computer interactions. This term insinuates that a state in which presence can be optimal exists. What "optimal" means in practice will vary according to context.

Why Presence? The justification for exploration into presence, requires examination of its opposing constructs: presenteeism and mindlessness. In most cases they are both approached from a health and wellness perspective. There are more extensive implications for both of these constructs when one considers the modern workplace, in particular, engagement. As both Langer (1989) and De Beer (2014) demonstrate, the best way to understand the need for presence is to explore the opposing constructs. Langer began with mindlessness and De Beer presenteeism.

Presenteeism. The global definition of presenteeism, according to De Beer (2014) extends beyond loss of productivity due to health impairment (health-related presenteeism) to include motivational aspects like boredom, challenge, or distraction (disengagement presenteeism). He points to numerous studies that reveal the cost of presenteeism is at least 1.5 times higher than that of absenteeism. Just because one shows up for work, it does not mean attention is here in the moment. Although the scope of De Beer's research is limited to the area of health-related presenteeism, he acknowledges the inclusion of disengagement presenteeism in the global context. For the purpose of this study, I will introduce a third form, based on mindlessness, called conscious presenteeism.

Hemp (2004) popularized the term presenteeism outside of medical literature. Hemp defines presenteeism as productivity loss resulting from real health problems. He discounts alternate forms of presenteeism. This could be an effect of the limited resource material and the two commercial studies for pharmaceuticals used. The studies' intent was to build a case for their products as a solution for lost productivity from illnesses such as allergy or depression. Others have built upon the definition (Chapman, 2005; Cooper & Dewe, 2008; De Beer, 2014; D'Abate & Eddy, 2007; Eddy, D'Abate, and Thurston, 2010; Tavares & Kamimura, 2014). This resulted in a wider use of presenteeism with qualifying terms and extension of its application beyond "real health problems."

De Beer (2014), an industrial psychologist from South Africa, identifies the difference between the forms of presenteeism as operational distinctions for researchers. I suggest there is a stronger association between these two forms of presenteeism. Some of the elements are inter-related to the psychological and their physiological counterparts.

Assigning a state to health-related or disengagement presenteeism does not consider the potential influence of the contemporary workplace. Increased need for treatment of stress and anxiety from fear of missing out (FoMO; Bragazzi & Del Puente, 2014) and mobile phone addiction (nomophobia; Archer, 2013) intersect health-related and disengagement presenteeism. I posit that a critical difference between the two is awareness of the impairment. What may be perceived as "working" or accessibility around the clock could be the cause of the presenteeism in itself. These factors are in addition to those already recognized by health-related presenteeism in the modern workplace: stress, poor diet, sedentary lifestyle, depression, and back strain (Ratey, 2008; De Beer, 2014).

D'Abate and Eddy (2007) extend the definition of presenteeism to include performing non-work-related activities at work, as non-work-related presenteeism. Their research instead sought to identify the individual and organizational implications of engaging in personal activities on the job. Non-work-related presenteeism overlaps with disengagement presenteeism.

Their research was conducted prior to widespread use of the smartphone and social media like Facebook and Twitter. Prior to the iPhone launch in 2007, access to the Internet was predominantly via the personal computer and in static locations. Individuals did not have access to the Internet in their pocket, as they do today through smartphones and extensive wireless and cellular network infrastructure. Nevertheless, their findings showed that significant losses resulted from non-work-related technology use (phone, email and Internet). The contemporary workplace has made technology indispensible for productivity and effectiveness. This needs to be taken into account. In addition, the advent of work-related activities not at work needs to be considered in the equation. In order to understand the extent of the impact of the ease of access on non-work-related presenteeism, further studies need to be conducted.

In D'Abate and Eddy's (2007) study, time spent with coworkers, clients, or work acquaintances discussing home or leisure-related issues is a contributing factor to presenteeism. The value of relationship building was not considered in their evaluation of these engagements. Their recommendations focus on the value of work-life balance. They do not take into account the value of relationships and effect on the ability to conduct and grow business.

Smartphones provide constant access to both work and non-work. D'Abate and Eddy (2007) identify the challenge of mixed life-worlds (home, work, and leisure). Boundaries between them are increasingly blurred as a result of the smartphone. FoMO and nomophobia unconsciously skew self-reported data collection by distorting the triggers for what requires critical attention. There is a sense of need or expectation for immediate response further blurring the boundaries.

In their follow-up study, Eddy, D'Abate and Thurston (2010) put a greater emphasis on the motivation rather than the impact. This approach identified convenience and boredom as the primary motivators. Convenience also has implications for ability to accomplish a critical non-work task without leaving work (saving productivity). Isolating the non-work-related actions derived from boredom and non-critical convenience motivation might render a more accurate measure of lost productivity associated with presenteeism in the contemporary workplace.

Mindlessness as Conscious Presenteeism. Mindlessness in the context of this study fits within the context of presenteeism as cognitive-presenteeism, loss of productivity due to actions without cognition (doing/responding without thinking). Cognitive intensive knowledge work needed for creativity, collaboration, and innovation are common in the contemporary workplace (Erlich, Bichard, & Myerson, 2010). Mindlessness, in the simplest form, is a state wherein one is not using the mind, cognition. This leads to unconscious response to our environment that blinds us to new possibilities (Langer, 1989). It is both a state and quality of a state in which people are unaware of their own judgmental state and therefore limited by their thoughts, emotions, or experiences in the moment. Mindlessness results in action and communication that is confined to an individual's unconscious response based on the past (Langer, Chanowitz, & Blank, 1985). The result of mindlessness is the potentially hindered personal development, organizational change, innovation, and learning required to accommodate the changing workplace.

Langer, a social and positive psychologist at Harvard University, approaches mindlessness as neither a negative nor positive state. Instead, her research shows that in a mindless state, flexible cognitive processing is absent. This might be demonstrated by the fact that one hears a direction, an automated response of a nod or even an action can occur, but the mind does not process the information actively. In the contemporary workplace, mindlessness is displayed regularly with automatic clicking on terms of acceptance forms without reviewing. Accidentally deleting important messages in overfull inboxes is another common act of mindlessness. Her argument is that the conditions dictate whether the brain responds with a cognitive response or a mindless one.

Evaluating one's state of presence is a challenge. The Langer Mindfulness Scale (LMS; Pirson, Langer, Bodner, & Zilcha-Mano, 2012) assessment tool is based on mindfulness as cognitive processing. It is one of the few mindfulness tools that consider the factors of engagement and innovation, critical in the contemporary workplace. As with the other tools, the capture and resulting data are based on a self-assessment. This has been a common concern with the existing mindfulness assessment tools, as they are primarily subjective. Evaluating presence or cognitive function based on self-assessment, one must also consider the ability of the participant to respond objectively in a potentially sub-optimal state.

Presenteeism and Mindlessness in the Workplace. Presenteeism, in general is a loss of productivity due to some form of impairment to presence. As with all previously mentioned variations of presenteeism, cognitive presenteeism should be considered relevant to the argument for presence in the contemporary workplace. They are not mutually exclusive either, as previously mentioned. Mindlessness could also be a result of health-related presenteeism. In other words, the cause of the response perceived as mindless may be health-related or disengagement rather than a lack of cognition. The mind is occupied with the pain or cause of stress, in which case, the behavior is not mindless, but rather not present. The variations in cause may overlap, but the outcome is lost productivity due to impairment to presence.

The interest of both presenteeism and mindlessness comes from two primary outcomes: lost productivity and engagement. Presenteeism is primarily recognized from the health-related (easier to measure) issues and the resulting high cost from lost productivity. Both can be identified for the psychosocial implications. Mindlessness, may be harder to ascertain as the measurements are primarily based on self-assessment. Understanding mindlessness in organizations began as a wellness concern (Langer, 1989; Kabat-Zinn, 2007), but is increasingly motivated by the productivity argument driven by conscious leadership and business scholars (Kofman, 2013; Reid, 2008, 2009; Senge et al., 2005; Tan, Goleman, & Kabat-Zinn, 2014).

The various approaches to defining impaired presence derive in part from the lens of the researchers. Langer's (2009, 2014) recent work in positive psychology views the balanced benefit to being cognitively engaged in the moment when needed, resting blissfully when not. De Beer (2014), an industrial-organizational psychologist, continues to look at the implications on productivity from burnout and stress. D'Abate and Eddy's (2007) research delves into the impact of non-work-related activities in the workplace as a human resource development (HRD) issue also acknowledging the need for balance, yet through a management science lens.

Further exploration into the causes of presenteeism is needed in order to find solutions that fit the contemporary workplace. None of the aforementioned researchers have considered the broader implications of the changing paradigm as it continues to evolve. The rise of the knowledge economy, and the ability to communicate and collaborate across the boundaries of cultures, disciplines, and functional areas (Friedman & Friedman, 2015) is a sign of this shift. Globally dispersed communities empowered by the Internet are able to share and work around the clock. Social technologies such as mobile devices, social media, video conferencing and other asynchronous tools enable such collaboration. The technologies used in the contemporary workplace change the "what," "when," and "where" of presence and affect our ability to "be" productive and engaged in the moment.

Presence in Organization Context. The contemporary workplace increasingly demands effective social interactions. Whether dealing with customers, managing a team, or negotiating terms for a partnership, the ability to be present in the moment can impact the outcome for both the individual and the organization. A greater need for social intelligence (Goleman, 2006) incorporating both social awareness and action is required for presence to be achieved. Once considered a soft skill, this extends the thinking beyond IQ and awareness of self to the people and organizations in which the engagement takes place. The coordinated energy of a human organization created something new and much greater than the sum of the individual energies of the persons involved (Saltonstall, 1959).

Leadership is not a solitary role, therefore awareness of self and other is critical. This requires active and deep listening while the experience of the moment unfolds. If we see it through the lens of Scharmer (2000), leadership as it pertains to presence is remaining focused on the here and now without influence of the past or future. Scharmer's presencing suggests that successful leadership is based upon the quality of attention and intention one brings to any situation. Within this context, collaboration has better outcomes. As a leader, this supports the needs of the evolving workplace dynamic where innovation requires inputs from all stakeholders.

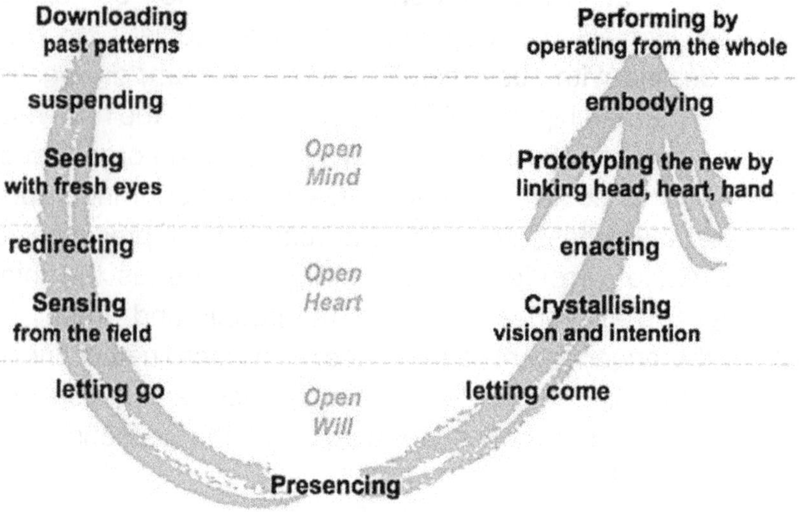

Downloading past patterns · Performing by operating from the whole

suspending · embodying

Seeing with fresh eyes · Open Mind · Prototyping the new by linking head, heart, hand

redirecting · enacting

Open Heart

Sensing from the field · Crystallising vision and intention

letting go · Open Will · letting come

Presencing

Figure 6. Theory U Diagram: Scharmer (2000, 2009). Adapted with permission of Presencing Institute - Otto Scharmer, www.presencing.com/permissions

Presencing as a process is expressed in Scharmer's Theory U diagram (figure 6) (2000, 2009), as the shift from seeing and sensing to presencing becomes open for new ideas (crystallization) and creation (prototyping). Notice the need for open will, heart, and mind at the various stages of the presencing process. Preceding presencing are stages related to self, followed by those related to other. Presencing is the threshold between letting go (self) and letting come (other), wherein one must be open and willing to trust one's self and other in the moment.

Executive presence (Hewlett et al., 2014) is unlike Scharmer's (2000, 2009) presencing in that it refers to the charisma, confidence, communication skills and appearance of the leader. Presencing involves an internal transformation. Executive presence can have an influence on whether one is perceived as a good candidate for leadership. Executive presence alone will not guarantee a leader is capable of leading in the contemporary workplace. On the other hand, the combination of executive presence and presencing fits the demands of this changing paradigm.

Mindfulness. Langer (1989) and Kabat-Zinn (2007) approached mindfulness differently from each other. The most pronounced difference is based on the approach to achieving a state of presence, mindfulness. Many scholars, Kabat-Zinn, and Brown and Ryan (2003) among them, profess the need for meditation to achieve a state of mindfulness. Mindfulness, in this context, is being aware and non-judgemental of self and moment. Kabat-Zinn is considered the man who brought mindfulness mainstream through mindfulness based stress reduction (MBSR). His work has made meditation and mindfulness more accessible to an audience beyond its traditional Buddhist roots. Meditation practices used by engineers at Google through a modified MBSR approach, accomplished in moments rather than minutes or hours, is a demonstration of this accessibility. In this context, the practice comes closer to Langer's mindfulness.

There is evidence that meditation is not the only answer to mindlessness. Langer's (1989, 2009, 2014) extensive research in preventative psychology demonstrates the ability to overcome mindlessness through various forms of practice, although not requiring meditation. Another approach or in combination, is supported by Ratey's (2008) extensive research in the area of exercise and the effect on the brain. Both Langer and Ratey's work support the wider range of alternatives to counter mindlessness and presenteeism without the requirement of meditation.

The role of mindfulness in organizations is increasingly visible through high profile organizations like Google, LinkedIn and Cisco. Leading the movement is Google's Search Inside Yourself Leadership Institute (SIYLI). These organizations have adopted programs that are leading to cultural change in leadership and business practices based on conscious leadership styles. This has a great deal to do with the concepts I have been mentioning thus far: attention and intention.

Optimal Presence. The concept of optimal presence was applied to psychotherapy by Morgan and Morgan (2005). Optimal presence describes the perfect conditions in therapy in which both client and therapist are "fully awake." It consists of the seven factors of awakening (the seven factors of enlightenment in Buddhist philosophy). Optimal presence assumes cultivation of awareness of the moment (attention) and those with whom it is shared (empathy) for the conditions to occur. Each of the factors provide the optimal conditions for being fully awake:

1. Mindfulness is being attentive to and awareness of the present.
2. Concentration is the most temporal in nature of the factors, as it refers to the being in and attentive to the moment.
3. Tranquility requires the quieting of inside voices as well as acceptance of what arises.
4. Joy is delight in the moment, also used in this context: happiness.
5. Energy is alert, yet relaxed, thereby creating a balanced state.
6. Investigation requires a curiosity for understanding the other.
7. Equanimity wherein the nearness to the moment and what it holds.

Mindfulness stands at the foundation of the seven factors of awakening. Awakening represents a shift in consciousness and action, whereas enlightenment connotes a final destination that is achieved (Nirmala, 2015). This is similar to the transformation in presencing. Mindfulness is a state of consciousness commonly defined as the state of being attentive to and aware of what is taking place in the present (Brown & Ryan, 2003), as illustrated in figure 7. Like awakening, mindfulness requires cultivation through attention and awareness. Although simplified in the illustration, in awakening and mindfulness, the state does not reside only in the head in the form of cognitive response to external stimuli.

Mind Full, or Mindful?

Figure 7. Illustration of mindfulness versus a mind full.

As a construct one might wonder whether there is a point or a state of optimal presence or whether the context dictates what is optimal. In both Morgan and Morgan's (2005) and Waterworth and Riva's (2004) use of "optimal" presence there is an assumed state. The primary difference in their definitions is that in psychotherapy optimal would assume suspending judgment. Waterworth and Riva suggest harmony between all aspects of self in order to be present in a moment, while suspending the idea of self, acceptance. I argue that these are conditions for optimal presence. There is no one state. It requires focus in attention and action with the context, yet there are conditions that apply to contexts of the state.

To explain my thinking further I propose a simple model, as seen in Figure 8. In both instances of optimal presence, one would attempt to achieve a state that is near the center, between self and other. In psychotherapy the upper half, awareness, of the model has greater emphasis. In human technical interactions, the emphasis would be on the lower two quadrants, engagement. In both instances there is a need for both self and other.

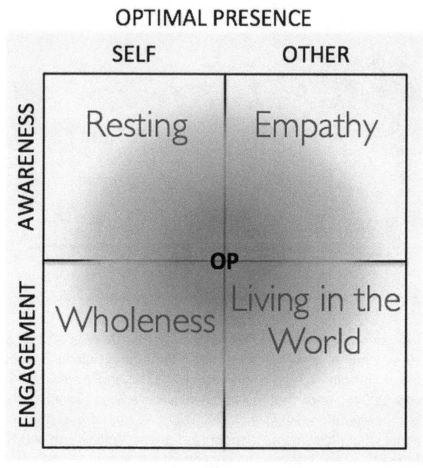

OPTIMAL PRESENCE

Figure 8. The states of the optimal presence model.

Presence is not passive in any form. It is dynamic and changing. It is suggested that one cannot maintain focus, the balance point, for greater than 3 hours daily. There are different contexts in which different states are optimal. Further exploration into the conditions of optimal presence for each quadrant of the model will provide insight into the dynamics of relations between people and organizations.

These four states are just a starting point from which the full model can be expanded upon in practice. In attempt to provide clarity in their intent, each state has been given a name. Note: the names for the states are not fixed and may change with further development of the optimal presence model. Examining the models further, one can see the potential to layer the Theory U diagram if the optimal presence (OP) model was flipped, the difference being that OP describes various states, rather than a process flow.

Applied. When applied to context of contemporary human and organization systems, presence as attention and intention has a common thread across disciplines. Just "being," "here," and "now" is no longer simple. Recognizing the cause and impact of the absence of presence is part of developing the solutions for improving presence in human and organizational systems.

There are five states of optimal presence based on the quadrant model: resting, empathy, wholeness, in-the-world, and balance. The first two, resting and empathy, relate to awareness. The second two, wholeness and in-the-world, relate to engagement. The fifth, balance, resides at the center between awareness of self and other as well as engagement with self and other.

Resting. The resting state of the first quadrant is introspective, not passive. This state is needed to either prepare for a shift or in recovery from change, approaching presence from kairos (opportunity) where kronos (time) is suspended momentarily to allow for metanoia (transformation) to emerge (Myers, 2011). The ancient Greek characters and concepts derived from them express the importance of the resting state for change to occur. The awareness of self opens the self to what it has to offer and what it needs. A period of deep listening and essentially breathing allows for gaining strength and compassion for self.

Empathy. The second quadrant is empathy wherein the focal point of awareness is shifted to other. In this state, suspension of one's self is necessary in order to become awake to the needs of other. It is a self-less state essentially. This state might be required to flow through a less desirable action with a desirable end of satisfying the need of the other. Affordances in change to enable suitable and mutually beneficial outcomes require the empathy state in stages of the change and negation process.

Wholeness. The third quadrant is wholeness, and involves engaging in active presence with self. This involves not only presence but also action, with caring for self. For the individual this might mean brain and body to build strength in the whole. Without a strong whole there is little to share and presence can suffer. For an organization it would involve caring for the people in the organization that make the whole and tending to the community that makes it strong. This state is critical to shift towards preparation for change or growth that requires strength and stability.

In the World. The fourth quadrant is expressed as a state of living in the world. This is a thriving cohabitation where engagement with others allows both to be better together than alone. This state insinuates a sense of being part of something bigger than self and other. It requires the systems thinking and a higher level of consciousness than the other three (even if only in context of the situation). This state is needed when a situation requires collaboration and openness. Living in the world is similar to Scharmer's (2000, 2008) performing state and Waterworth and Riva's (2004) extended self.

Balance. These four states are just a starting point from which the full model can be expanded upon in practice. In attempt to provide clarity in their intent, each state has been given a name. Note: the names for the states are not fixed and may change with further development of the optimal presence model. Examining the models further, one can see the potential to layer the Theory U diagram if the optimal presence (OP) model was flipped, the difference being that OP describes various states, rather than a process flow.

Social Technologies

Social technologies have brought new meaning to presence through social presence. Social presence is the adaptive mechanism that enables the Self to identify and interact with the Other by understanding the other's intentions within a virtual context (Waterworth & Riva, 2014), presence as described by Waterworth as the ability to put intentions into action. Asynchronous interactions manipulate the temporal construct as well as physical separation which enable co-creation of one's perceived presence. In this case, the co-creation is the unique sense of what is here and now, based upon the contextual interpretation and representation of two or more individuals. They suggest that to achieve maximal presence, one must suspend self-consciousness. In order to be fully present, one must neither judge themselves nor be concerned about being judged by others. Social presence requires trust and shared context.

In interactions mediated through technology, the opportunity to filter or edit one's actions and appearance to create perceived optimal presence exists. Imperfection and spontaneous responses can be replaced by airbrushed images and scripted responses. This is not unlike executive presence from leadership, which requires more charisma than authenticity or self-awareness. In the world where mediating presence through technology, mastery of the tools can simulate a perceived perfect image of presence: physical, attention, and intention.

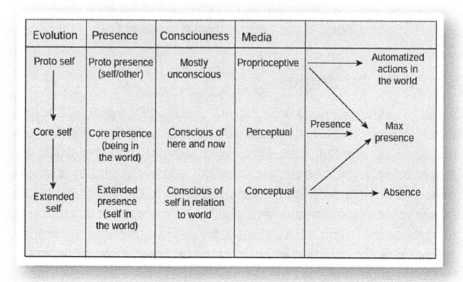

Evolution	Presence	Consciouness	Media		
Proto self	Proto presence (self/other)	Mostly unconscious	Proprioceptive		Automatized actions in the world
Core self	Core presence (being in the world)	Conscious of here and now	Perceptual	Presence	Max presence
Extended self	Extended presence (self in the world)	Conscious of self in relation to world	Conceptual		Absence

Figure 9. Presence: Layers, media and mental states (Riva et al., 2004). Reproduced with permission

Riva, Waterworth and Waterworth (2004) explain the human ability to experience presence as an evolutionary function of the nervous system that enables us to differentiate between internal and external states. As illustrated in Figure 9, the proto self is the self versus non-self. The core self is the state in which one is able to use conscious selective attention to interpret the here and now in its current context. The extended self is the recognition of the significance of self in the world. The absence of core and extended presence is Langer's (1989) mindlessness, desirable in certain contexts to rest and recover sense of self. Suspension of self-consciousness, the proto-self, enables the maximal presence they suggest is needed in mediated interactions. Integration of the three presence states accommodates for different contexts needed for survival.

They experimented within presence in the design context using focus, locus, and sensus. Focus is the degree of integration of the three layers. Locus is the degree to which the individual is engaged in real world versus virtual. Sensus is the attentional arousal that can lead to emotional or physiological response. Sensus integrates embodied presence as experienced in both conscious and unconscious states; for example, the experience of immersive virtual reality gaming platforms in which the player commands a virtual environment through movements triggered by other sensory (sight, movement, and sounds) cues.

Although Riva, Waterworth and Waterworth's (2004) work take place in mostly virtual and blended context they provide a window into the challenges that occur in the contemporary workplace. For example, Cisco and IBM have remote workers with consistent tele-presence. They use video conferencing technologies that constantly stream of remote employees' workspaces. Distributed academic programs like Fielding Graduate University use the tools for training, curriculum delivery, communication, and relationship building with students and faculty. Medical procedures are performed remotely using wearable technologies like GoogleGlass to provide the visual and audio streaming of patients and their vitals. The contemporary workplace is driven by the knowledge economy and the tools needed to connect it. Waterworth and Riva (2014) write a thorough and compelling theoretical work on presence in the face-to-face and blended world of today.

Social presence enables the self to identify with other developing the capacity to understand the intentions. This is essential in mediated environments such as social media or even mobile texting when the context is not always clear. Riva, Waterworth and Waterworth's (2004) definition of social presence is "being with other Selves" in a real virtual environment. It is from social presence, that optimal presence occurs, in this case networked flow. In networked flow, each party perceives social presence, a shared state of transformation resulting in shared outcomes and actions to make them happen. These characteristics represented are as optimal in presencing in leadership (Scharmer, 2000; Senge et al., 2005) as well as mindfulness in change work (D'Abate & Eddy, 2007; Langer, 2014).

Witnessed Presence. In technologically mediated interactions, presence takes on some variations to its characteristics. After all, when presence is asynchronous the temporal sense is modified. When one is physically in a different space for the interaction, the spatial element is also manipulated. Yet, presence is what is perceived. Society is somewhat stuck in the perception of present-in-person paradigm. The concept of witnessed presence, as introduced by Nevejan and Gill (2012), involves developing trust in merged realities. Witnessed presence is a bridge between containing intention, availability, embodiment, representation, culture, imagination, and fictional presence. In order for trust to emerge, the four factors of time, place, action, and relation is the extension of present-in-person temporal and spatial definition. Social Strategy. Social strategy as a field has rapidly come to the forefront in the last decade as a result of the changing demands of the contemporary workplace. Technological advances influenced how and where communications take place and relationship management occurs. This extends beyond the role of marketing and communications to all levels and areas of organizations and individual communications (Mishra & Evans, 2009: Bingham & Conner, 2010). The rules have changed and traditional leadership models are challenged (Li, 2010: Li & Solis, 2013). Augmenting relationship management of both face-to-face and online connections has become a critical skill for value creation (Forbes Öste, 2009, 2013: Rubin, 2014). Application of social technologies in organizations is not the question, but rather best practice for their ability to enhance potential rather than hinder.

Social Optimization, the Balance Point. The additional factor of optimal presence in my model of the four quadrants would be the focal point, balance. This point has the characteristics of reciprocity and trust. The basis for this comes from the foundation pieces presented in the practice of social optimization. This methodology evolved from my years of social strategy work. The basic premise of social optimization, is the building and maintaining of mutually beneficial and effective relationships (Forbes Öste, 2009, 2013). "mutually" being the bridging concept that brings these two constructs together. In order for the states of awareness and engagement to simultaneously occur with optimal presence, trust and reciprocity is maintained between self and other. A high level of social intelligence (Goleman, 2006) is required for balance to be maintained, wherein the social awareness and facility are in sync.

Trust and reciprocity require the presence to be aware of not only what one has to contribute (or lose) but also what the other has to gain or lose from an interaction. Molm (2010) describes the potential impact of reciprocity to not only counter negative effects of power inequality, but also to lead to efforts to change the structure of power. The effect being the potential for impact on both the endurance of relationships and also the stability of networks in which the exchange takes place. This is expressed in the "maintaining" element of social optimization that recognizes that relationships evolve over time. Because one is fully present in one exchange does not assume that this is true of future or past interactions.

Social Media. In the context of social media, image and presence are often reflected as brand. How we wish to be perceived and the image we actually project are often different. What is "real" and even what that means can be obscured by the mediated quality of editing. Turkle (2011) professes that the unedited life is most fulfilling Much of what is shared is touched up, revised, and even removed via filters. Whether through our own or paid PR firms that project the perfect image of person and company, it is changed. The implications for trust and self-image for both the sender and receiver are challenges in themselves. Layered upon this are the various tools and the context in which the elements of self should appropriately reside. Each individual (and organization) is complex, but that is part of the beauty.

Chapter 2 Summary

In this chapter we have explored the theoretical underpinnings of wearables and presence in the workplace. Examining the complexities of design theory and behavior change will hopefully provide some insight into the design-based findings derived from the study. Exploring presence theories showed us how presence of mind is required to bring one's best self to the workplace. Expanding the framework for what might be considered optimal presence in the workplace situates the use of presence and changing forms. Lastly we looked at the shifting paradigm as a result of social technologies in the contemporary workplace. A relationship-based system with an increasing emphasis on human relations requires presence. Now, let's look at the method for exploring the connection between all three in the study and how they relate to the question and subquestions: Are there affordances from wellness wearable technologies that correlate with sense of presence-of-mind in the workplace? What are the potential design and user challenges when adopting wearable technologies for undesirable behaviors modification or health-related impairments? What is the potential impact of wearables' use on presenteeism and mindlessness in the workplace? Is there a correlation between wearables technologies and quality of social interactions, related to self-assessed sense of presence with others? Is there a correlation between increased awareness of self from the physiological to the psychosocial (through wearable data and experience)?

CHAPTER THREE

METHODOLOGY

Objective

The objective of this research was to explore correlations or other indications of relationships between use of wellness wearable technology and the user's sense of presence in the contemporary workplace: being conscious and aware in the moment.

People in the contemporary workplace come in many shapes and sizes, cultures, generations, and states of wellness. They are exposed to stress, physiologic and psychological, as well as life and system challenges. Technology has both aided and influenced these changes. The prevalence of wifi, laptop webcams, and mobile phones renders any connected location a potential workplace regardless of physical or geographical constraints. New technologies are designed to enhance social, physical, and cognitive capabilities. The physiological consequences of too many hours sitting are harmful to both the individual and the organization (Carr et al., 2015). Anxiety and even obsession with keeping connected disrupts sleep and attention (Edwards, Jones & Cunningham, 2014). Bodies deteriorate from lack of movement, sunlight, poor posture, stress, depression, sleep-deprivation, and poor diet. The relationship with humans and technology and how they evolve together in the contemporary workplace is part of this story.

There is a bright side too. In the emerging category of wearable technology there are some potential solutions. This study explored the affordances of wearables as interventions for issues that hinder presence in the contemporary workplace. After all, if everyone is suffering from pain, depression, obesity, and distraction, society will surely be in a disconnected sad state. Yet, each of these limitations (when not severe) has a potential remedy. There is solid scientific research behind the connection of the body and brain that lead to development of each of the wearable technologies used in this study. The future is far from bleak if people and organizations learn not only to adapt but also to thrive.

Research Design

This study utilized a mixed methods approach to capturing and analyzing the data. The first phase was quantitative using a validated self-assessment tool for mindfulness with a particular focus on presence. This was administered using an online survey tool and results analyzed using statistical software. The second was in the form of interviews coded into themes and analyzed both manually and using software for accuracy and effectiveness in identifying findings.

Participants. The demographic of the participants targeted mid-career professionals. The age range is 40-65, although some outliers (early Baby Boomer and early Millennials) also fit the other criteria. Recruiting for the study was done through social media and social network channels. This invitation was extended via personal and professional networks both in social media, such as LinkedIn groups as well as direct email to the link from the http://forbesoste.com/research website. By using social technologies as the means for recruitment, it was assumed that respondents to the call were active using such methods for communication. To currently measure results in the contemporary workplace is to measure in a connected workplace. Recruiting participants comfortable with social technologies limited potential challenges based on digital literacy for the tools being used. As a result, the participants are representative of the changing culture of organizations where social technologies have a value outside marketing and branding (Mishra & Evans, 2009; Bingham & Conner, 2010).

Recruiting through my personal and extended networks, there are risks for limiting diversity of thought in the participants. Having worked as an expat for the larger portion of my career, my network is quite culturally diverse. That said, the U.S. based portion and particularly the Bay Area group is both particularly tech savvy and interested in consciousness. This has the potential to impact the results, and must be noted to avoid generalizing the results to the larger population.

SurveyMonkey™ hosted the recruitment survey which filtered out participants that did not fit the study demographic. For the purpose of ease in distribution of devices, it was limited to recruiting of U.S.-participants. Distribution of devices was prioritized to local addresses in the San Francisco area for the purpose of follow up and retrieval, although more than half required shipping. That said, in both rounds, the participants represent a contemporary global workforce as many of them are expats in the US or Americans working on globally dispersed teams.

Each stage of the study sought to contain a participant group of 50 participants. The target number of participants, 100 total, was selected to get ample data for validation of the results. These were spread across devices to be sure of no greater than 20 and no less than 5 participants per device type, to avoid meta data skewed to a particular device or user. The pilot started with 50 participants, 40 of whom completed the duration of the study. The adjusted final study began with 58 participants, 36 of whom participated in the full duration of the study. The issue of attrition will be discussed later in the findings.

The demographic spread of study participants in the final group, adjusted based on findings from the pilot, is seen in Table 1. The larger group of female participants registers the fact that one of the devices was gender specific. The intent was to target mid-career professions which is reflected in the number of participants in the Baby Boomer and Generation X groups.

Table 2

Demographic Distribution of Final Study Participants

| | Gender | | Generation | | | | Workplace | | |
	Female	Male	EBB	BB	X	M	Onsite	Onsite & Remote	Remote
GENDER									
Female	33	-	2	6	15	10	10	17	6
Male	-	25	1	4	13	7	8	12	5
GENERATION									
EBB	2	1	3	-	-	-	0	2	1
BB	6	4	-	10	-	-	3	4	1
X	15	13	-	-	27	-	7	13	8
M	10	7	-	-	-	17	8	8	1
WORKPLACE									
Onsite	10	8	0	3	7	8	18	-	-
Onsite & Remote	17	12	2	6	13	8	-	29	-
Remote	6	5	1	1	8	1	-	-	11
Totals	33	25	3	10	27	17	18	29	11

During the registration process, participants were asked to select a category of wearables function that would be of most interest to them based on their needs. Several participants had prior experience with fitness bands or pedometers. These individuals were matched with a different category of wearable to ensure a new experience, and to match with their requested function. For example, they were assigned a pain management or posture correction wearable. The categories were issue based: pain management, fitness, posture, stress, mood, focus, and sleep. The wearables were assigned accordingly to first or second choice, as available.

The demographics collected were generation, gender, and workplace status as seen in Figure 10. The generations were defined using the Pew Research guidelines (Fry, 2015): early Baby Boomers (1945-1954), Baby Boomers (1955-1964), Generation X (1965-1980), Generation Y (1980-1992), Millennials (after 1993).

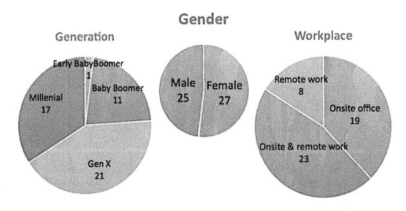

Figure 10. Demographics of participants by generation, gender and workplace. (graphic reflects all participants from start of the study).

Defining the characteristics of midcareer professionals in today's global workforce comes into question when designing a profile for participants of this study. Despite our 99.5% shared human genetics (International HapMap 3 Consortium, 2010), experience defines us. Human behavior changes with the demands of the environmental and cultural factors (Ehrlich, 2000). The contemporary workplace is one such crux moment in which one is required to stand out in order to stand together. Recognizing one's unique strengths and sharing them for effective collaboration is valued. This leads to anomalies as the norm rather than the anomaly (Forbes Öste, 2013). That which is perceived as the norm is actually the anomaly. Midcareer professionals from the contemporary workforce are quite diverse, and it is just this diversity that makes them who they are as a demographic. Social strategy places value in diversity, but also recognizes it as a challenge for universal communication when using shared platforms with global audiences.

Using my extended network has some interesting challenges regarding seeing marked results. I am physically active and many in my extended network are equally so. The individuals attracted to the fitness trackers were already active, but interested in quantifying and augmenting. Many pilot participants came from the extended Fielding network, in other words, PhD students and PhDs. The experience of becoming a PhD in the social sciences involves a great amount of self-awareness and evaluation. Were they fully present, perhaps not (especially if in the middle of writing their dissertation)? As noted earlier, the movement toward valuing greater self-awareness and consciousness in organizations is gaining traction with the help of Google, LinkedIn, and events like Wisdom 2.0 for Business. As an active participant in this community several participants came from this network as well.

Lake (2011) reflects on this dichotomy when describing the scholar's tendency to place other scholars in particular schools of thought, but claiming they themselves cannot be categorized. Mid-career professional and even workplace norms are not as clearly defined as they were pre-Internet and mobile telephony. With so many factors to take into account, one must recognize the impact on the results if the anomalies are the norm.

Procedure. The study used mixed methods of quantitative (survey data, text-based interviews) and qualitative (Skype™, video conferencing interviews and narrative inquiry). Changes in users' sense-of-presence scores were evaluated and tracked through self-assessments on SurveyMonkey™ while adopting assigned wearables with functions related to the user's desired function or issue. The interviews that followed the device use phase provided feedback on their experience with the wearables as it related to their ability to be present.

The presence (self-awareness and awareness of self with others) research involved an online survey. The Mindful Attention and Awareness Scale (MAAS-short; Brown & Ryan, 2003) was used to self-assess presence weekly. MAAS-short was selected based both on its extension validation and on its focus on presence, and inclusion of self and other elements. The design uses a Likert scale response of frequency (always to never) as follows:

1. Difficult to stay focused in the present
2. Doing jobs or tasks with awareness
3. Being without much awareness of what is done
4. Doing things with paying attention
5. Doing jobs or tasks automatically
6. Easy to stay focused in the present
7. Listening to someone doing something else at the same time
8. Doing things without paying attention
9. Being aware of what is done
10. Listening to someone without doing something else at the same time

Participants were assigned and received wearable devices at the commencement of the study with instructions for use and set-up as well as overview of the study procedures. Local participants received them directly, and the rest were sent via trackable post. While waiting for their devices, participants completed an online survey (hosted on SurveyMonkey.net™) weekly starting one week prior to receiving the device to establish a baseline. The results were analyzed using IBM's statistical analysis software, SPSS™. The survey took less than 2 minutes to complete. Reminders were sent via email to participants at varied times to ensure continuous participation. The survey ran for 7 weeks (with devices, therefore 8 weeks total).

After completing the study, participants complete an exit interview to capture their experiences with presence (engagement with self and self with others). The interviews were conducted using email. Some of the participants were asked to expand upon their experiences via a call using Skype™ or GotoMeeting™.

The qualitative portion of the study consisted of the interview questions distributed via email. The questions were designed to be open ended to encourage more extensive response than yes or no. The questions 1-4 relate to a particular quadrant of presence as is described in the optimal presence model (Figure 9): Self-Awareness (Resting), Other-Awareness (Empathy), Self-Engagement (Wholeness), Other-Engagement (In the World). Question 5 was intended to clarify affordances related to the wearable that could have impacted the results. Question 6 was used to understand the participants' adherence to the guidelines of the study, in regards to device usage. Question 7 was intended to clarify additional factors or conditions that could have impacted the results. The questions were as follows:

Please provide examples of observed change / or lack thereof):

1. What change(s) did you experience in self-awareness during the course of the study?

2. What change(s) did you experience in your awareness of your ability to be present with others, both how you felt and how you were received?

3. What change(s) did you experience in your engagement with yourself (i.e., taking care of) during the course of the study?

4. What change(s) did you experience in your engagement with others during the course of the study?

5. Please describe any factor(s) that may have contributed/inhibited your presence of mind as a result of use of wearable technology during the study.

6. Did you use the wearable regularly as required for the duration of the study? Would you continue to do so?

7. Additional information: Any information in the context of presence of mind that might have influenced your responses outside of the study (during the time of the study) would also be helpful. Disclosure of private details not necessary category is fine, i.e. family challenges, moving, health issue...

Upon approval of this dissertation by the committee, participants received a report. The report included both the overview of the research findings as well as their personal results.

The Devices. The devices in this study were either donated by or on loan from manufacturers for research purposes only. Each device was limited to no less than 5 units and no more than 20 to avoid skewed results based on one device or one user. The purpose of the study was not market research or device comparison, but rather understanding of the outcomes beyond performance function. There was no monetary exchange accepted. The benefit to the manufacturers was to increase the knowledge outcomes from their products, where there is a dearth of research. The agreement with the manufacturers provides access to the results limited to the scope of the study. In addition to the final report, manufacturers will be provided results from users of their device with regards to presence and feedback, if volunteered. Demographics are provided for further understanding of the data. Individual identifying information is not made accessible to the manufacturers. The device and its accompanying app data are not accessed for the purpose of the study. It is not within the scope of the study and belongs to the participant in terms of privacy.

	Fitness & Sleep	Fitness	Multi	Mood	Pain	Posture	Focus
						Device Function	

	Fitness & Sleep	Fitness	Multi	Mood	Pain	Posture	Focus
GENDER							
Female	8	4	2	10	4	1	4
Male	12	4	2	0	0	3	4
GENERATION							
EBB	2	1	0	0	0	0	0
BB	3	3	0	3	0	1	0
X	10	2	1	4	2	2	6
M	5	2	3	3	2	0	2
WORKPLACE							
Onsite	5	3	1	2	1	3	3
Onsite & Remote	10	5	3	4	3	1	2
Remote	4	0	0	4	0	0	3
Devices distributed	20	8	4*	8	4*	4*	8

*totals in chart do not include devices distributed with no data collected.

Table 3.

Device distribution by function and demographic

The intent is to derive metadata from the study and not to focus on one particular device or device type. The device selection is based on functions that apply to potential presence inhibitors as follows: pain, fitness, focus, depression, posture, stress, and sleep. Some of the devices have overlapping functions in these categories. They were assigned based on interest or need of the participant as identified in the registration for the study. The distribution by demographics for the final study was as shown in Table 3 above. The grouping of the devices and their users are shown in Figure 11.

Devices

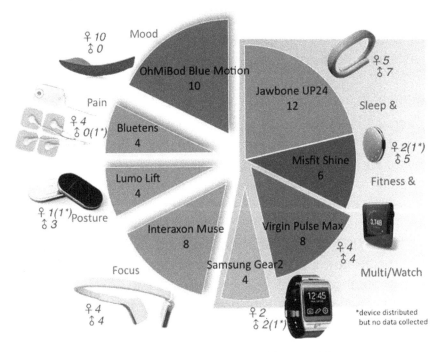

Figure 11. Wellness wearables used in
the study and their groupings

Fitness. Intellectual stimulation, or exercising of the brain, is shown to result in healthier and more active cognitive function and even stimulation of brain cell growth, neuroplasticity (Robertson, 2000). Brain math, Sudoku, and reading are known to keep the brain not only vital but generating new connections in mature adults (Kukekov et al., 1999). The synapses continue to grow and new cells are generated. In his book, Spark, John Ratey (2008) refers to several studies that support exercise's positive effect on stress reduction, depression and focus, and even neurogenesis. The levels required vary per individual.

The studies support the theory that even 20 minutes of exercise a day (even just walking) can stimulate the brain by releasing the

BDNF and serotonin the brain needs. In other words, you do not need to be a marathon runner in order to get the physical benefits and happiness benefits of exercise. Health club memberships have long been part of employee incentives programs. We are now seeing these programs providing incentives to use wellness wearables. Organizations increasingly are prioritizing wellness as it is good for productivity, and therefore has implications for the return on investment in their employees.

Exercise is known to be good for our physical health, but the effect on the brain is an area of cognitive neuroscience that is receiving a lot of attention as of late (Ratey, 2008: Bergland, 2012). Escalating problems with inactivity and our lack of movement are resulting in rising levels of obesity and type 2 diabetes (Buck, 2009). These may be physical conditions, but they are very real and can have neurological side effects related to stress, depression, and focus (Ratey, 2008). Obesity and depression often present together, causing debate with relation to both correlation and/or causation. That is to say that being active is both physiologically and psychologically beneficial.

Fitness wearables are designed for improving one's physiological health through greater awareness of self in movement, sleep, dietary intake, and in some cases heart rate and breathing. The data are captured by both sensors on the devices and by input from users. In addition, most of the devices have a social component on the accompanying smartphone app. Social exercise provides an additional augmentation to the experience by limiting the isolation often associated with inactivity and depression (Cohen & Janicki-Deverts, 2009) The social feature connects them to others using the device and/or health care providers to give feedback.

In 2014, all the major smartphone platforms launched health data aggregator tools. Apple launched Healthkit™ in June of 2014 for all iPhone™, iPad™, and AppleWatch™ users. Google Fit™ (Google), S Health™ (Samsung), and Nudge™, a standalone that aggregates the data from various wearables, are easily accessible for all smartphone users. Earlier health data aggregators were primarily the domain of the early adopters of the quantified health movement.

Worth noting again is the limited accuracy of the sensors at this point. In general, they provide data to present a picture of activity levels rather than the precise amount of movement. When I tested devices for use in the study, worn simultaneously, three different devices produced three widely different results. In addition, most of the devices do not register an intensive hour of yoga or bicycling. This type of activity does not trigger the accelerometer (the technology inside which tracks movement). As a result, dependent on the activity type, the user may be required to manually enter his or her activities. This is somewhat defeating the purpose of the device for some users. In the interviews of pilot participants, this led to a high level of frustration with the device. One participant stated, "I found it frustrating that the total results missed the greatest exertion, climbing Tuckerman's Ravine. It registered incorrectly. I didn't even meet my goal." Note that Tuckerman's is an 8.4-mile hike up 4,300 feet.

The scope of this study includes inquiry into whether physiological self-awareness induced by using wearable technology affects psychological self-awareness and ability to be present in the moment. The purpose is not to compare devices and their sensors for their accuracy. I mention it because some of the participants refer to these issues in regards to their experience during the course of the study. To overcome these issues as distractions in themselves further exploration of the root causes from the user experience is needed.

The fitness wearables used for this study are Jawbone UP24™, Misfit Shine™, and VirginPulse Max™. Each of these devices has slightly different features. All three are in the fitness category with movement (steps and sleep). The accompanying apps track calorie intake and allow for adjustments to activity for this not registering on the devices. The UP24™ has vibration alerts for alarms and idle time. These devices are worn 24/7 through the course of the study, as they monitor sleep patterns as well.

Chronic Pain. "Chronic pain is considered a persistent type of pain lasting for three months to six months or longer, and lingers beyond the 'normal' expected course for healing," according to Dr. Danoff of the American Osteopathic Association (2015). Chronic pain can range from mild to severe, continuous or sporadic, merely uncomfortable to totally incapacitating. According to the Gallup Healthways Well-Being Index in 2013, 47% of Americans suffer from chronic pain. The emotional toll of anxiety, depression, and fatigue that accompany chronic pain contributes to presenteeism (Langley et al., 2010). Pain is often managed with medication that can further inhibit focus and presence.

The device used in the study is a wearable transcutaneous electrical nerve stimulation (TENS) unit, BlueTens. Unlike the fitness bands that are based on sensors, TENS devices send stimulating pulses across the surface of the skin and along the nerve strands. A TENS device is used for nerve-related pain conditions (acute and chronic conditions) and has the added benefit of stimulating the body's natural pain relief source, endorphins. The BlueTens™ is user controlled via a smartphone app. These devices are used daily for the duration of the study.

Additional pain management wearables were lined up to be included in the study, but launch delays prohibited them from inclusion. This was in part due to the device requiring FDA approval based on its health claims (Patel, 2015). The approval both requires validation studies of the effects and also enables the device to be categorized as a medical device (and therefore covered by insurance). It was also due in part to production challenges. At the time of the study, the BlueTens™ units used were pre-launch and first version, as was the accompanying application.

Focus and Stress. Focus has a more obvious relationship to presence. Although focus is less of a physical trait, it can be trained through brain exercise (Gates & Valenzuela, 2010: Jhansi & Krishna,

1996). It is from this angle that the electroencephalography (EEG) wearables technologies approach focus. Stress reduction is often coupled with this functionality in wearable devices. Stress manifests in both physiological and psychological symptoms. Gone untreated, stress can lead to high blood pressure, heart disease, obesity and diabetes (McEwen & Stellar, 1993). The chart below from the Mayo Clinic ("Stress symptoms: Effects on your body and behavior," 2015) outlines the most common effects of stress (Table 4).

Table 4.
Stress Symptoms: Effects on One's Body and Behavior (Mayo Clinic, 2015)

... On your body	... On your mood	... On your behavior
Headache	Anxiety	Overeating or
Muscle tension or	Restlessness	undereating
pain	Lack of motivation	Angry outbursts
Chest pain	or focus	Drug or alcohol
Fatigue	Irritability or anger	abuse
Change in sex drive	Sadness or	Tobacco use
Stomach upset	depression	Social withdrawal
Sleep problems		

Interaxon's Muse™, the EEG monitoring headband used in the study, is one such device. It trains the brain using EEG sensors on the forehead that manipulate a game on a smartphone or tablet as brainwaves change from calm to stressed. Participants were recommended to do the Muse training daily throughout the course of the study.

Mood. Mood is challenging to track outside of a controlled lab and often subjective. In the case of finding a wearable for the study, a particular cause of mood change was selected. In this case, hormone-related depression and moods in women was the focus. According to the Mayo Clinic, one in five women develop depression and it is most common between the ages of 40 and 59.

This is within the age range mid-career professionals used in the study, and therefore provides a good fit. Oxytocin is a neurochemical that can affect happiness (Bergland, 2012) and is referred to as the bonding chemical. Oxytocin is shown to increase empathic reactions (Bartz et al., 2010), which are much needed for the other-awareness in optimal presence. The wellness benefits of oxytocin beyond depression relief as follows: stress reduction, pain relief and improved sleep (Komisaruk, Beyer-Flores, & Whipple, 2006) are also compatible with the presence inhibitors in the context of this study.

Oxytocin is stimulated through physical contact from cuddling to sex. Studies using oxytocin inhalers on lab animals have proven effective in triggering the pro-social effects of the neurotransmitter (Yamasue et al., 2012). For the purpose of this study a connected (as in Internet via Bluetooth or wifi via a smartphone) wearable was needed for triggering the body's natural release of oxytocin. OhMiBod's wearable vibrator called BlueMotion™ complied with the requirements of the study. The BlueMotion™ device was assigned to women who self-identified as suffering from hormone-related depression or moods.

Each individual is different in the frequency of and quantity of oxytocin required for the effects of oxytocin to remain after the initial release of the hormone. The initial recommendation from a sexologist was anywhere from 3x daily to 4x weekly. In addition there was the need to account for women's menstruation cycles. The adjustments were made to accommodate these conditions. The women were requested to use their devices a minimum of 4x weekly. They could pause the study during their cycles and resume when it was over. In addition they were asked to complete the presence assessment within 24 hours of using the device.

Posture. The Alexander Method (Brennan, 1996) puts a great deal of emphasis on posture as a path to well-being and success. The method originally grew out of the need for perfect posture in acting and performance. The Alexander Method has been widely adopted in occupational health for improving employee well-being and performance. The method is a form of coaching that teaches body and spine awareness and training to improve the use of the body.

The body language of posture has negative and positive effects. The non-verbal communication of poor posture is both negative to self and other (Scheflen, 1964). The benefits of power posing (Cuddy, Wilmuth, & Carney, 2012), intentional open stances build self-confidence. Training body awareness to maintain upright posture gains better eye contact and impacts other as well as self in terms of optimal presence and the ability to engage effectively.

For the purpose of this study, two posture training devices were planned for use in the study. The LumoLift™ is worn throughout the day on the lapel or bra strap. It vibrates as a reminder to correct posture. The UpRight™ is worn for a 15-minute training session daily, and sticks to the lower spine. Users were asked to use as recommended by the manufacturer due to the variations. Both have accompanying smartphone apps. In the end, the LumoLift was the only posture device used in the study, due to launch challenges of the UpRight (now resolved) at the time of the study start.

Sleep. Participants that identified with sleep issues were assigned fitness devices with sleep features. These devices had varying features such as the following: track and report sleep patterns, power-nap alarms, vibration alarm based on REM, physical and/or auditory alarms. For this functionality, users were required to wear the devices at night, and in some cases to activate sleep-mode on the device in order for the tracking to be accurate. In particular the Up24™ and Shine™ have specific sleep functionality (some or all of the features listed above).

The Sleep in America 2008 report was commissioned by the National Sleep Foundation using a random sample of 1,000 participants working 30% or more. Among the findings were that 29% of respondents have fallen asleep or became very sleepy while at work in the past month because of sleepiness or a sleep problem.

Twenty-six% reported daytime sleepiness interfering with their daily activities at least a few days a week.

Much research in the area of sleep has been done in recent years. Sleep, as a wellness priority, is a focus in Arianna Huffington's book, Thrive (2014). Her interest in sleep issues developed out of her own health challenges. She suffered from extreme burnout, which was identified as the detrimental effect of sleep deprivation and stress. She became involved with several scholarly sleep studies and institutes as a result. She has been a bit of a poster child for the importance of sleep ever since. Her advocacy and thrive index has been adopted by many corporate wellness programs, and particularly the inspiration for Virgin Pulse Institute.

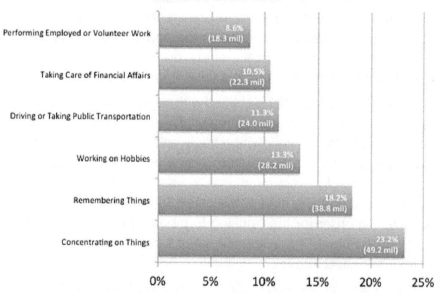

Self-reported Sleep-related Difficulties Among Adults ≥20 Years
2005-2006 & 2007-2008

Figure 12. CDC, Sleep-related difficulties among adults

The National Center for Chronic Disease and Prevention and Health Promotion (CDC, 2014) declared insufficient sleep a public health epidemic following the release of study results from Institute of Medicine and the National Center on Sleep Disorders Research in 2009. The recommendation from the National Sleep Foundation for good sleep habits referred to as sleep hygiene are as follows:

- Same bedtime each night and waking time each morning.
- Avoid large meals before bedtime.
- Avoid caffeine and alcohol close to bedtime.
- Avoid nicotine.

Using wearable technology that can alert to bedtime and wake times can potentially train the first habit. Tracking of the other three can be done through many of the accompanying wearable apps to build awareness and hopefully train the user for better sleep hygiene. For the purpose of the pilot, two devices with sleep and consumption behavior tracking are used, the UP24™ and Shine™.

MAAS: Reliability and Validity.

Brown and Ryan (2003) developed the Mindful Attention Awareness Scale (MAAS) in a 15-item format. They initially demonstrated its utility to predict motivational and wellbeing outcomes. Among their studies, they showed that changes in MAAS-measured dispositional mindfulness pre- to post-intervention correlated with declines in mood disturbance and stress in participants in a mindfulness based stress reduction (MBSR) program. The MAAS has since been proven to be as reliable in the 10-item version (that used for the purposes of this study). As the purpose of this study is non-clinical, the concern for a clinically validated instrument is not as relevant. One area to note is the sensitivity of the MAAS individual differences in mindfulness training. The participants in my study are mid-career professionals, many of whom are based in California, where contemplative practices are commonplace. In particular, many who expressed interest in participating already had an interest in mindfulness. This will need to be taken into consideration when looking at the data particularly at the baseline.

Höfling, Moosbrugger, Schermelleh-Engel, and Heidenreich's (2011) adaptation of the 15-item MAAS to the 10-item version used in this study was validated in a comparison study with both versions and the additional Kentucky Mindfulness Scale (KIMS) subscale Acting with Awareness (AWA). The adaptation has the added feature of mirrored items, positively rephrased. The results showed that not only was the shorter version as reliable, but even more consistent with regard to AWA.

Measures and Instructions.

MAAS-Short

Item	Characterization of item content
maas3(–)	Difficult to stay focused in the present
maas7(–)	Being without much awareness of what is done
maas10(–)	Doing jobs or tasks automatically
maas11(–)	Listening to someone doing something else at the same time
maas14(–)	Doing things without paying attention
maas3(+)	Easy to stay focused in the present
maas7(+)	Being aware of what is done
maas10(+)	Doing jobs or tasks with awareness
maas11(+)	Listening to someone without doing something else at the same time
maas14(+)	Doing things with paying attention

Scoring System for Measures. Based on a mean of all items, MAAS scores can range from 1 to 6. Higher scores indicate greater mindfulness. In the context of the study, the intent was not to determine whether the participants have high or low scores. Instead, the change in score from baseline (pre-device use) was observed.

The Pilot

Phase 1 was conducted as a pilot study. There were 50 participants each assigned one of the eight devices available for the first round. Participants completed the presence assessment prior to using their wearables to establish a baseline. They were requested to begin familiarizing themselves with the devices and using them once the baseline assessment was complete.

As is expected in mid-career and mid-life, "life happens." Life is expected to happen during the course of this study, both in the workplace and out. The intention with optimal presence is to be aware of "life happening" and to be there mentally when it does. When several of the participants moved mid-course, this was noted, but they continued the study.

Despite the bumpy start, 46 of the 50 completed the study. The results from the MAAS assessments were all over the place. The pilot ran at the end of 2014 beginning of 2015. The slow start was a result of delays in device distribution and launch. Noted for the final study, avoid major holiday periods and provide more detailed guidelines on use in terms of the study to avoid ambiguity.

The pilot had twice weekly presence assessments for 5 weeks. Nearly all of the participants were still in an early adoption phase after the 5 weeks, where the device use itself was not a part of their "regular" routine. The final study was changed to once weekly for 7 weeks to allow for more time to adjust to the devices and less influence of the survey itself. As each group underwent the same treatment, observing change by device type accommodated for change potentially resulting for the assessment alone, particularly when patterns of change are seen by device or device type.

Data Analysis

The results of the survey were downloaded from SurveyMonkey. net™ and then loaded into SPSS for clean-up and then evaluation. Scores were tracked over time initially establishing a baseline (pre-device), then Week 1 through Week 7 (with device) , as shown in Figure 13. User data were filtered by device and to identify if there were particular differences based on device types and demographics to identify any patterns in response changes.

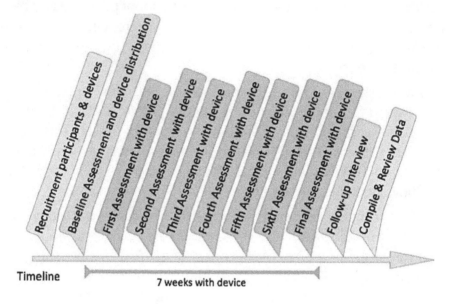

Figure 13. Study timeline

The MAAS-Short is a widely used assessment tool for measuring mindfulness. The selection of the short version was made based on tests showing that not only was it as effective as the full version, but in some cases even more effective (Brown & Ryan, 2003) for the assessment of mindfulness in the context of presence of mind. The challenge in mindfulness assessment is the subjective nature of the concept. Using a self-assessment can provide insight into perceived mindfulness, but cannot provide a fully accurate gauge as to one's mindfulness. It is therefore qualified within this study one's "sense" of self and "sense" of self with others.

Note: In addition to the standard MAAS scoring, items 2, 4, 5, 7, 8, and 10 were coded in this study for awareness of other (things and beings), while 1, 3, 6, and 8 were coded for awareness of self.

The primary analysis of the survey data was done using a one-way analysis of covariance (ANCOVA) to observe changes in MAAS score while accommodating for baseline (pre-use of wearables) scores. This was also used to look at the results by the moderator variables (gender, generation, or other demographics) and specific devices/categories of devices to identify statistical significance based on these additional variables. By running each of these, the influence of the covariates will be explained. The test of between subject effects resulting from this analysis will provide information on the significance of the results. This will be important in order to validate the results.

Additional analysis was done by breaking down the questions to apply to the optimal presence model to identify patterns. Baseline scores and (week 7) final scores were used to observe change from pre and post intervention. This was done using a two-way ANCOVA. The secondary survey analysis accounts for the awareness of self and self-with-other scores to observe if the changes are weighed in one particular direction. The tertiary analysis of the MAAS scores for "doing" and "being" as applies to engagement was also done. The splitting of MAAS questions by theme for analysis is not a tested method, and therefore may introduce more questions than answers. Nonetheless, it could provide grounds for more extensive research in the future.

Chapter 3 Summary

The intent of this study was to explore the relationship with wearables and presence in the workplace. As wearable technology is a new category that is evolving rapidly, there is much opportunity for exploration beyond the scope of this study in outcomes. Even within the current scope, further exploration could be done with more updated or different devices. That said, given the constraints and the moving target as this field evolves, it is critical to start somewhere with exploring the potential of these devices in the workplace. This approach provides an opportunity to explore the hidden affordances as well as the perceived affordances of wearables as they pertain to presence in the workplace.

CHAPTER FOUR

FINDINGS

Participation

This section provides the findings of both the quantitative and qualitative results from the study. As seen below (Fig. 14), the participation was not consistent throughout the study. Some of the discernable reasons will be discussed as part of the findings where relevant to the study. For the purpose of integrity in the quantitative data, the complete scores were used for the overall meta results.

Nonetheless, the intent of the study was to observe the change in scores from baseline to 7 weeks of usage. As such, in the meta-context, the results in the final study include all 36 participants who reported both the baseline and week 7, variability in between is not recognized. Changes in scores were evaluated both as those who completed the study from baseline to week 7, and as a whole to observe trend lines.

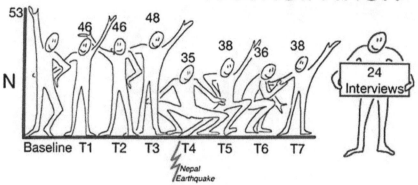

Figure 14. Surveys and interview responses received

Quantitative Results from MAAS

The one-way repeated measures ANOVA was conducted to compare scores on the MAAS being at time 1 (prior to the use of wearables), time 1-7 (and one week intervals while using the wearables). The means and standard deviation are presented in Table 5 (descriptive statistics, below). There is no significant effect for time, Wilks' Lambda =.763, F (7,17) =.753, p >.001, multivariate partial eta squared =.237.

Table 5.

Descriptive Statistics of Wearables and Presence Study MAAS Mean Scores.

Descriptive Statistics

	Mean	Std. Deviation	N
MAAS Score Baseline	3.1642	.34242	24
MAAS Score Wk1	3.1000	.44134	24
MAAS Score Wk2	3.1042	.36413	24
MAAS Score Wk3	3.0713	.40776	24
MAAS Score Wk4	3.0842	.38665	24
MAAS Score Wk5	3.1413	.28109	24
MAAS Score Wk6	3.2542	.44329	24
MAAS Score Wk7	3.1246	.43429	24

The MAAS assessment is based on a Likert Scale from 1-6. The estimated marginal mean MAAS scores at the baseline were only slightly above the 3.5 center point. The change over the course from the start of the study (T1) to week 7 (T8) was < 0.2.

The participation in the study was not consistent resulting in 24 of 58 participants who completed all surveys on time in correct sequence. The results in the top layer of Figure 16 demonstrate the change from baseline to week 7 including participants who did not complete all assessments (but did complete the baseline and week 7) providing a before and after intervention reading.

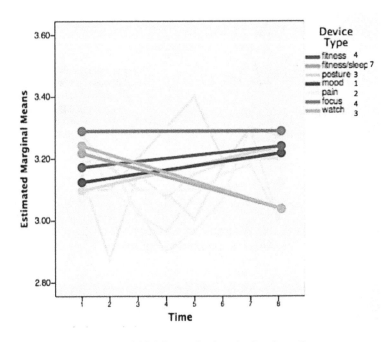

Figure 15. MAAS results by device function,
before and after intervention

Upon examination of the estimated marginal means of MAAS scores applying the moderator variables, the patterns are similar in returning to within 0.2 points of the baseline measure. The exception being Baby Boomers with a decreased mean score by under 0.4

points or 6.7% change. That said, neither produced results that were statistically significant.

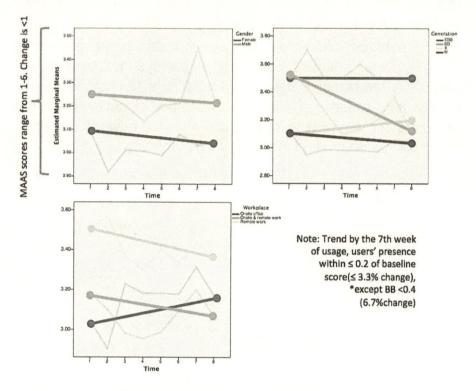

Note: Trend by the 7th week of usage, users' presence within ≤ 0.2 of baseline score(≤ 3.3% change), *except BB <0.4 (6.7%change)

Figure 16. Wearables and presence study
MAAS means by demographics

The above charts (Figure 16) show the change from baseline to week 7 without the influence of other variables. Introducing the other variables produces slightly different results; although still not statistically significant, they are of interest to notice in comparison. The chart in Figure 17 provides insight into the direction and degree of change dependent on the moderator variables with their covariates. The graphs are aligned horizontally to compare the variation in mean scores on the same scale. The largest degree of change and variation in score is shown in the generation grouping. Slight variation in the workplace, smallest effect in remote workers.

Even smaller difference observed in the mean scores by gender, despite slightly different starting points.

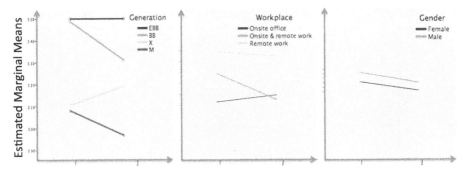

Figure 17. Wearables and presence MAAS means by demographics with covariates.

Quantitative results for optimal presence

By isolating the mean scores on questions with particular context as previously outlined are filtered as follows: Self-Awareness, Other-Awareness, Being-Engagement, Doing-Engagement, additional patterns emerge. This is also influenced by analysis in isolation versus with their covariates. In Figure 18, the analysis demonstrated the influence of the covariates on the mean results.

The variables in isolation are not used for the optimal presence diagrams of the remaining variables; instead the graphs shown represent the changes in estimated marginal means for each of the four quadrants: self, other, being, and doing, as related to presence when under the influence of covariates. The representation in isolation does not represent a real world situation and as such should only be used for statistical analysis when combined.

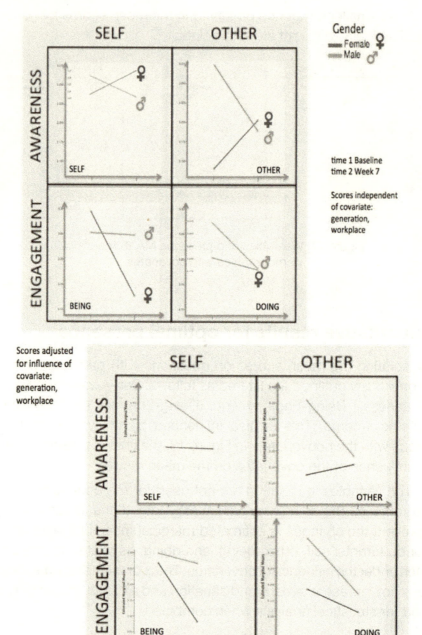

Figure 18. Comparative MAAS based on moderator variables in isolation versus with covariates.

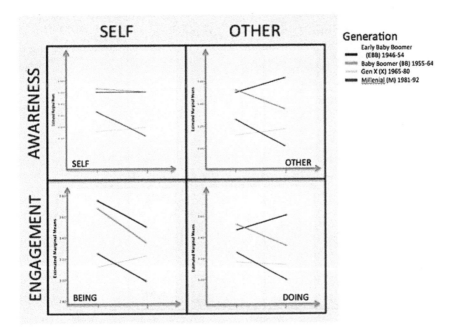

Figure 19. Change in estimated marginal means of MAAS questions separated by presence forms applied to generation.

The change in MAAS means by questions type in presence forms (Figure 19), displays an observable difference in response to the intervention by generation. The scores still are not of statistical significance, but the trend lines are more distinct. Millennials show a consistent decrease in scores on all areas of presence. Generation X presence scores remain nearly unchanged. Baby Boomers' mean scores in all quadrants decrease, with the exception of self-awareness, which is unchanged. The early Baby Boomers show the greatest variation in increased awareness of and engagement with Other.

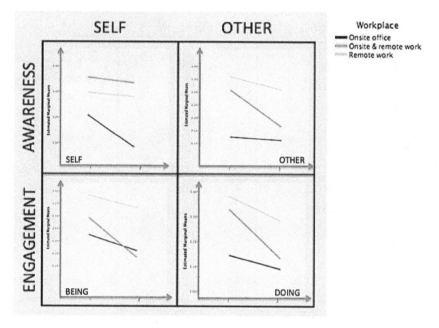

Figure 20. Change in estimated marginal means of MAAS questions separated by presence forms applied to workplace.

Workplace, much like generation shows a more distinct difference in the response to the intervention (Figure 20). Remote workers are mostly unchanged in all quadrants. Onsite workers experienced the greatest shift in decreased self-awareness, even so this being <0.1 point change. Participants who work in a hybrid environment of both onsite and remote showed the largest shift in all areas except self-awareness, which remained unchanged. That said, at its greatest amount, this was only <0.2 points. Without doing a much larger study over a longer period of time, the results are inconclusive, but worth potential further investigation.

Findings from Qualitative Measures

Upon completion of the final survey, the participants completed a questionnaire used as an exit interview. Some participants were also asked to do a follow-up interview. The resulting responses lead to the following findings.

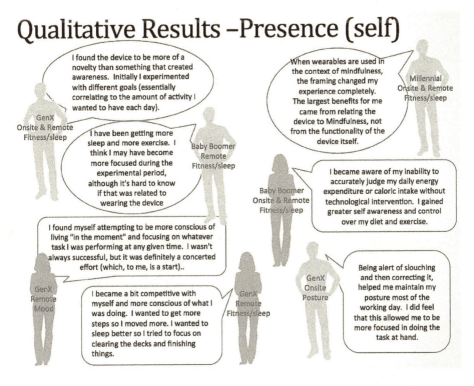

Qualitative Results –Presence (self)

I found the device to be more of a novelty than something that created awareness. Initially I experimented with different goals (essentially correlating to the amount of activity I wanted to have each day).

GenX Onsite & Remote Fitness/sleep

I have been getting more sleep and more exercise. I think I may have become more focused during the experimental period, although it's hard to know if that was related to wearing the device

Baby Boomer Remote Fitness/sleep

When wearables are used in the context of mindfulness, the framing changed my experience completely. The largest benefits for me came from relating the device to Mindfulness, not from the functionality of the device itself.

Millennial Onsite & Remote Fitness/sleep

I became aware of my inability to accurately judge my daily energy expenditure or caloric intake without technological intervention. I gained greater self awareness and control over my diet and exercise.

Baby Boomer Onsite & Remote Fitness/sleep

I found myself attempting to be more conscious of living "in the moment" and focusing on whatever task I was performing at any given time. I wasn't always successful, but it was definitely a concerted effort (which, to me, is a start)..

GenX Remote Mood

I became a bit competitive with myself and more conscious of what I was doing. I wanted to get more steps so I moved more. I wanted to sleep better so I tried to focus on clearing the decks and finishing things.

GenX Remote Fitness/sleep

GenX Onsite Posture

Being alert of slouching and then correcting it, helped me maintain my posture most of the working day. I did feel that this allowed me to be more focused in doing the task at hand.

Figure 21. Wearables and Presence Interview responses (self)

Participant responses (Figure 21) in relation to self-awareness demonstrated the challenge of measuring one's sense presence, a subjective concept, as well as what might be influencing it. Participating in a "wearables and presence study" triggered participants to initially have anticipated effects, due to suggestion. This can be a result of the Hawthorne effect (Landsberger, 1958), also mentioned in the Human Cloud study (Rackspace & Goldsmith, 2014), wherein participants' behavior or outcomes are not directly attributable to the treatment but rather as a result of their awareness of being in a study. In this study, understanding this effect also provides useful data when exploring potential interventions and actions.

Several participants expressed the subjective nature of their response to the study in their interviews. As one participant explained, "I have been getting more sleep and exercise. I think I may have become more focused during the experimental period, although it is hard to know if that was related to wearing the device." Another declared, "the largest benefits for me came from relating the device to mindfulness, not from the functionality of the device itself." And a third stated, " I believe just knowing I was doing the study made me present (or try to be) but was unrelated to the specific device I was trying."

The functionality of the devices targeted particular presence inhibitors, although not all required behavior change. Three of the five categories of wearables functions target behavior modification in order to get the desired effect. Behaviors trigger notifications for the user to self-modify and retrain the behavior while tracking and charting within an app. The exceptions were the mood and pain management devices, which actively stimulate nerves for the desired functional effect.

Participants noted awareness of behavior change in several interviews. "I became more competitive with myself and more conscious of what I was doing. I wanted to get more steps so I moved more. I wanted to sleep better so I tried to focus on clearing the decks and finishing things," said one participant. "Being alert of slouching and then correcting it, helped me maintain my posture most of the working day. I did feel that this allowed me to be more focused in doing the task at hand," said another. A third explained the human computer interaction of his partnership with the device by stating, "I became aware of my inability to accurately judge my daily energy expenditure or caloric intake without technological intervention. I gained greater self-awareness and control over my diet."

The pilot participants had more to say about the observed behavior change. One said, "I was able to improve my sleeping pattern and amount during the course of the study, so I rarely felt overly fatigued, and I think I was more present because of that." Another stated, "I became more aware of my actual activity level and my actual sleep level. Both of those contributed to being more satisfied with what I did over a 24 hour time period." A third shared, "I slowly increased my good posture hours from 0 per day to my best of 4 hours per day."

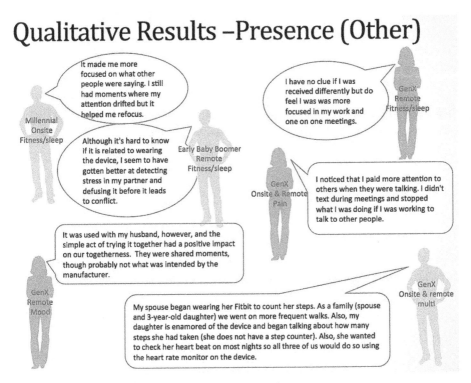

Figure 22. Wearables and presence
interview responses (other)

In relation to changes in their perceived presence with others, participant responses (Figure 22) reflected feedback loops from interactions. By observing their own behavior or thoughts, they adjusted accordingly. One said, "when people lost their tempers or seemed distracted, I began to notice it more and contrast my own behavior in response." Another shared, "I definitely became more aware and when I slept well and took better care of myself, I was more clear in my thought and articulation. For the days I was off balance, I felt enough of a presence to realize it and minimize my business actions with clients."

The effect of sharing of data or the wearable experience on participation was also noted in the interviews. When devices were assigned to known groups or pairs the partners were asked to reflect. Four participants in the pilot remarked on the change in their partner's ability to manage stress and focus after using the Muse™. One participant reflected that competitiveness in a mindfulness application was counter to the function of focus: "I got a bit competitive with my husband, who was also participating in the study with the Muse. The measurement aspect was not good for me, so we stopped comparing how well we did (how many 'birds' we got)." The shared experience of the BlueMotion™ depended greatly on the individual and the partner from "the simple act of trying it together had a positive impact on our togetherness" to "made me too powerless for my comfort level."

Competition was noted in the shared experience. In the final study there was a group of five colleagues assigned the same fitness/sleep device. They stated that competition with their peers motivated their participation in the full study and to achieving daily goals, which required behavior change. Another participant using the Gear2 said, "My spouse began wearing her fitbit™ to count her steps. As a family (spouse and 3-year-old-dughter) we went on more frequent walks. Also my daughter is enamored of the device and began talking about how many steps she had taken (she does not have a step counter). Also she wanted to check her heartbeat on most nights so all three of us would do so using the heart rate monitor on the device."

Perceived status that impacted interactions came out in several of the interviews as well. "I felt special to be wearing my red UP24TM and was aware of my feelings of superiority relative to non-initiates. I perceived myself to have augmented personal aura in most one-on-one interactions, and projected thoughts of respect and even envy onto casual passers-by - while at the same time being aware of the absurdity of these projections." Another said, "I brought more enthusiasm to outings but I don't think it was appreciated for others who didn't have the device." A third shared, "I found myself fidgeting with the device sometimes. People asked about it and then I had conversations about having more awareness."

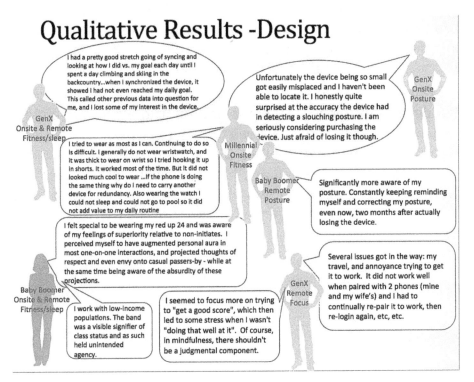

Qualitative Results -Design

I had a pretty good stretch going of syncing and looking at how I did vs. my goal each day until I spent a day climbing and skiing in the backcountry...when I synchronized the device, it showed I had not even reached my daily goal. This called other previous data into question for me, and I lost some of my interest in the device.

GenX Onsite & Remote Fitness/sleep

I tried to wear as most as I can. Continuing to do so is difficult. I generally do not wear wristwatch, and it was thick to wear on wrist so I tried hooking it up in shorts. It worked most of the time. But it did not looked much cool to wear ...If the phone is doing the same thing why do I need to carry another device for redundancy. Also wearing the watch I could not sleep and could not go to pool so it did not add value to my daily routine

I felt special to be wearing my red up 24 and was aware of my feelings of superiority relative to non-initiates. I perceived myself to have augmented personal aura in most one-on-one interactions, and projected thoughts of respect and even envy onto casual passers-by - while at the same time being aware of the absurdity of these projections.

Baby Boomer Onsite & Remote Fitness/sleep

I work with low-income populations. The band was a visible signifier of class status and as such held unintended agency.

I seemed to focus more on trying to "get a good score", which then led to some stress when I wasn't "doing that well at it". Of course, in mindfulness, there shouldn't be a judgmental component.

Unfortunately the device being so small got easily misplaced and I haven't been able to locate it. I honestly quite surprised at the accuracy the device had in detecting a slouching posture. I am seriously considering purchasing the device. Just afraid of losing it though.

GenX Onsite Posture

Millennial Onsite Fitness

Baby Boomer Remote Posture

Significantly more aware of my posture. Constantly keeping reminding myself and correcting my posture, even now, two months after actually losing the device.

GenX Remote Focus

Several issues got in the way: my travel, and annoyance trying to get it to work. It did not work well when paired with 2 phones (mine and my wife's) and I had to continually re-pair it to work, then re-login again, etc, etc.

Figure 23. Wearables and presence
interview responses – design

Findings related to design relate to the following: the devices themselves, their accompanying apps, and operating instructions related to the user experience (Figure 23). For example, "Since it's small, wearing it all the time, including at night is not a big deal." The majority of the negative feedback had to do with lost connection between their device and their smartphones, sensors limitations, and user interface of the accompanying smartphone application. Small pieces, missing or forgotten chargers and accessories, pairing devices with phones, lack of (or unclear) instructions for use, and generally fitting it into one's routine and "look" are all inherent challenges of the new category of wearables that were also identified in the interviews. "The instructions for use were very cursory ... I found myself frustrated to understand the various capabilities of the device. Perhaps the instructions are meant to be cursory to prompt users to experiment, but I still would have appreciated more detailed information." Another said, "The machine did not connect well to my phone and often times needed to be restarted during a session."

Fifteen participants either dropped out of the study after losing the devices (or pieces of), could not get it to work, or were not comfortable with continued use (Table 6); typical of the 30% abandonment rate (Lazar et al., 2015) of wearable devices. One user shared, " I did use it very regularly, until I lost it about 5-6 weeks in... The following morning I have to get up early to fly overseas. It was not until I arrived at the other end that I discovered that it was missing."

Table 6.

Study Completion and Attrition by Demographics and Device Type

	Complete	Base & wk7	Baseline	≤Wk 1	≤Wk 2	≤Wk 3	≤Wk 4	≤Wk 5	≤Wk 6	Total
GENDER										
Female	10	5	4	1	3	5	1	1	2	33
Male	12	7	2	0	0	1	1	0	1	25
GENERATION										
EBB	1	0	0	0	2	0	0	0	0	3
BB	4	2	0	0	1	3	0	0	0	10
X	10	8	5	0	0	2	0	1	2	27
M	8	2	1	1	0	1	2	0	1	17
WORKPLACE										
Onsite	8	8	8	0	1	2	0	1	2	18
Onsite & Remote	12	5	5	1	2	2	2	0	1	29
Remote	4	5	1	0	0	2	0	0	0	11
DEVICE										
Fitness/Sleep	8	6	2	0	1	2	0	0	0	20
Fitness	3	0	1	0	1	2	0	0	0	8
Multi	3	1	0	0	0	0	0	0	0	4
Mood	1	2	0	0	1	3	1	0	2	8
Pain	2	1	0	1	0	0	0	0	0	4
Posture	3	0	0	0	0	0	0	0	1	4
Focus	3	2	2	0	0	1	0	0	0	8
Totals	24	12	6	1	2	6	2	1	3	58

Regarding the study, one participant expressed frustration with her expectations of the study based on no direct perceivable connection between the wearable and presence. "My wearable was not designed as a device to make the user more present in any way. If anything, it is a distraction from the tasks at hand and I am unsure why it was utilized in this particular study." This will be discussed further in the next chapter, as it relates to expectations and hidden affordances.

Qualitative Results - Life

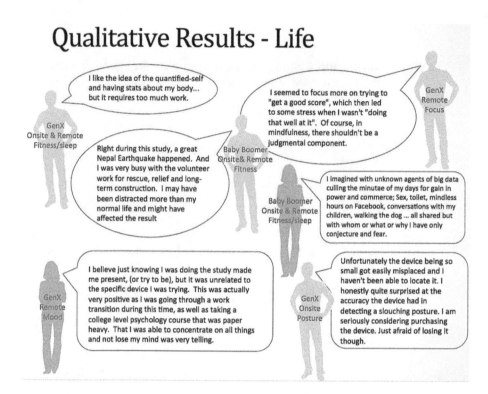

Figure 24. Wearables and presence interview – life

The human factor of integrating devices into already complex lives can make adoption of anything new a challenge. Life happens (Figure 24), especially as a mid-career professional where one is attempting to balance career, family, health, and community. The community aspect of life was emphasized in the midst of my study when a large portion of my participants became involved in the rescue efforts resulting in the Great Nepal Earthquake. Others had more personal catastrophe in the form of relocation, divorce, or passing of a loved one. Just one more thing to manage often results in lost devices or lack of commitment to change.

Chapter 4 Summary

The study on wellness wearables and sense of presence in the contemporary workplace was intentionally done in the real workplace. It was not a controlled environment, and as such the complexities of it were considered in the findings. The concept of workplace is also evolving and as such, the conditions in which work takes place and the tools used with them. This study provides a glimpse into the potential challenges in determining interventions for presenteeism. What is apparent from the findings is that it is often a combination of things that can influence presence.

This study indicated that presence, based on self-assessed tools, did not increase or decrease significantly during the adoption of new wearables. In the 7-week quantitative study, presence scores normalized to within 0.2 points of starting point. Qualitative interviews presented additional information about the interaction of the two interventions: wearables and the presence assessment. The social factor of users who participated together using the same device limited attrition from the study (and continued use of the wearables). The neurotransmitters (i.e., serotonin, endorphin) responses as a result of device use (i.e., increased blood flow from increased activity, decreased pain from corrected posture or tens stimulation) were not apparent enough to the user to register in the given self-assessment measures for presence. Presence as an affordance introduces an additional level of complexity to measurement, as it requires exposing the hidden and unconscious behavior and mind.

CHAPTER 5

DISCUSSION

Discussion

There is increasing interest in wellness and presence by organizations and individuals. Exploring emerging technologies as potential interventions to counter presenteeism (health-related, disengagement, and conscious) contributes to this body of knowledge. Wearable technologies continue to mature and become more integrated into our tech and life ecosystems. As they mature, so too will the understanding of sociomateriality (Orlikowski, 2007; Orlikowski & Scott, 2008; Leonardi, 2013; Parmiggiani & Mikalsen, 2013; Fagan, 2014; Gaskin, Berente, Lyytinen & Yoo, 2014) and the interdependence between user, technology, and the ecosystem in which they reside. There is a need to further understand the indications and implications of sociomateriality when exploring emerging technologies as applied to the contemporary workplace.

Implications

The implications of this study and accompanying review of literature expose the need to explore the relationship between emerging technologies and the environments in which they are adopted.

Presencing in leadership (Scharmer, 2000; Senge et al., 2005) recognizes sociomateriality as a factor in the future of presence both as an influence and as a new reality. Wellness and presence are connected to the human experience (Waterworth & Riva, 2014). Successful design is related to the experience not the product (Rowland et al., 2015). The contemporary workplace requires developing trust in merged realities as it is neither a controlled environment nor fixed in the temporal or spatial sense (Nevegan & Gill, 2012).

Sociomateriality. Sociomateriality is a growing field of inquiry to explore the relational ontology wherein the socio (i.e., humans and organizations) and material (i.e., technology) are fused. I approached sociomateriality from a critical realism lens, which assumes the two entities are separate until fused through human interaction (Leonardi, 2013). As opposed to Orlikowski's (2007) agential realism approach, in which the two are inextricably related (one does not exist without the other). Sociomateriality suggests the properties of technology are entangled with social norms, individual interpretations, and work flows (Parmiggini & Mikalsen, 2013). As proposed by Leonardi and Orlikowski, future research and dialog must recognize the fusion of the sociomaterial as opposed to the isolation of the elements. By taking sociomateriality into account, discourse on design, presence, and social strategy are placed in the context of the contemporary workplace.

There is rapid development and launching of new and improved devices and applications in the category wellness. Recognizing when sociomateriality occurs and the affordances (both perceived and hidden; Norman, 2009) of that fusion needs to continue as the change occurs. Affordance and constraints are perception of utility or impediment as a result of the sociomaterial fusion. Emphasis on the experience over the product (Solis, 2015) in design and application will lead to increased mutuality. The personal nature of wearables relies on embodied immersion (Waterworth & Riva, 2014) in which the elimination of the boundary between self and the technology allows for the fusion or sociomateriality to occur. Hoshi's (2012) human experiential design explains it as that need for design (technology) to be embedded into the experience, disappearing from perception.

The more personal the device is, the more it becomes recognized as both physically and psychologically as part of a new entity. The fitness band and the person become a health-conscious person, similar to networked flow where the perceived social presence becomes a shared state of transformation in which shared outcomes and actions are a result of the fused entity. It is therefore of less value to evaluate in isolation, as it is the combination of actors not the individual entity that creates the experience.

Mediated presence (Waterworth & Riva, 2014) has increasingly sociomaterial fusion wherein the awareness of the experience is of greater relevance than the medium. The means is transparent and the outcome is presence. Creating or identifying the perfect conditions in kairos (opportunity) and kronos (time) in optimal presence allows metanoia (transformation) to occur, but requires context in the contemporary workplace.

The user experience design is critical part of design intended to influence behavior (Fogg, 2007; Wendel, 2014). Fogg's persuasive design model uses simultaneous motivation, ability, and trigger. Wendel's action funnel model involves feedback loops for refinement of the change. Both were reflected in this study. Fogg's model has been put to practice in the development of several of the devices used in this study as was shown in the findings. Participants who suffered from poor posture and back pain (motivation) used the posture training wearable. A notification (trigger) occurred when posture was compromised. Users extended their spine to their baseline (ability) good posture. Wendel's (2014) model takes the action beyond the moment or single action of persuasion to continuous behavior change. In the case of this same device, lost components inhibited participants' ability to continue use. The responsiveness of the manufacturer to replace lost components allowed the participants to continue with minimal pause. The feedback loops provide continuous input relevant to the user and technology's context as they evolve.

Considering sociomateriality for successful sustained persuasive design would allow for a greater understanding of the fused entity that is the user and device(s) within its ecosystem of the contemporary workplace. Change and persuasion occurs not because of the technology or the user, but rather the fusion of the two within the context. This study suggests the benefit of further exploration of both models to identify when and if sociomateriality occurs. Without achieving sociomateriality, the motivation for sustaining the behavior change (device use) is minimized, as the device and the user remain separate entities. Both models emphasize the need to understand the user's experience. Neither Fogg nor Wendel assume that a state of sociomateriality is achieved, but rather refer to a behavior change as a response to stimuli under certain conditions.

It is therefore critical to continue doing studies that use devices in real conditions rather than labs. Norman (2009) and Rowland et al. (2015) emphasize the need for understanding the changing landscape, social intelligence, and other human and workplace factors. These rapidly evolving conditions impact the user experience as a critical component in supporting future products, particularly wearables. Early devices, such as were used in this study, provide insight into the context as it relates to user needs and device limitations for future development (both anticipated and actual) as they evolve. Real world studies recognizing the anomalies of the contemporary workplace, such as this can identify how best to develop, design, and implement such tools and their accompanying actions for greatest benefit.

Wearables. Wearables are an example of such a tool. Studies on influence of wearables on behavior are subject to the expectations of anticipated or desired results. Integrating this into the understanding of actions and tools used as well as the context of the individual provides a wealth of data on how to combine interventions and effective duration of treatments. The Human Cloud Study (Rackspace & Goldsmith, 2014) attributed a degree of results affected by the Hawthorne effect (Landsberger, 1958) from which the act of being observed influences the results. Similar to the use of placebos in pharmaceutical interventions, the result may be psychosomatic, as are some of the presence inhibitors themselves. The resulting behavior change influenced by expectations or by virtue of being observed indicate potential opportunities. Developing future interventions with a social or reporting element might use this effect as a motivator in itself for the behavior change and/or sustaining it. For example, some of the participants using the same devices who checked on each other also had more complete participation in the study.

Early product abandonment or lack of sufficient usage is often the result of lack of clarity in user guidelines, instructions, or poor user interface and surfaced in this study. The eternal beta of Ship-It (Richardson & Gwaltney, 2005) for crowd-sourcing product development feedback is widely accepted with emerging technologies. While the wearable category is still considered emergent, users' expectations need to be set accurately. Wendel's (2014) action funnel model takes this into account. Despite the complexity of the model, it would be worthwhile for manufacturers of future devices to consider integrating in all the stages, even post-distribution.

Improved efficiency in power, form factor, and connectivity will naturally remove barriers already identified in this study such as convenience and lifestyle. Real life distractions influence adoption of devices and ability to habituate them into routines. Perceived problems of size (loss of pieces or devices), maintenance (power source, water resistance), and comfort (sleep interruption, sharp edges, size) may increase frustration and therefore contribute to presenteeism. The challenges in this area were also findings in the Wilson (2013) and The Human Cloud (2013, 2014) studies. This shows the continued opportunity for improvement in power, form factor, and connectivity. Understanding the real world experience of users and identifying opportunities to improve as the technology evolves should result in better design solutions beyond the challenges of wearability (Rowland et al., 2015). Understanding the human factors as well as the changing landscape of the contemporary workplace are critical components when developing new products and services (Norman, 2009, Rowland et al.).

Well-Being. Self-assessment tools alone are not sufficient for evaluating presence and its impact on presenteeism in its many forms (D'Abate & Eddy, 2007: De Beer, 2014). Expectations around the concept of presence and self-awareness influence results when introducing an intervention with self-assessed scoring (Langer, 1989). As in other areas of wellness, it is not simply diet or exercise in isolation, but rather a combination that takes lifestyle-behavior change to create the desired effect (Ratey, 2008). Complementary experiences, such as the survey in this study or personal mindfulness practices, also potentially influence the results.

This study contributes to the understanding of presenteeism as it corresponds to the contemporary workplace. Presenteeism can no longer be treated as solely a health-related or distraction issue, but rather must include the conscious presenteeism. This wider definition allows for the overlap of hindrances and requirements that challenge today's workforce. The World Health Organization (WHO, 1948) includes physical, mental, and social in well-being. It is critical to recognize the relevance of treating the physiological, psychosocial, or environmental disruptions to ability to bringing one's best self to work.

Exploring wellbeing programs in organizations that recognize the broader definition of well-being as a part of the contemporary workplace mediator variables would provide an interesting future study. Other interventions that cross over the physiological to psychological and consciousness-based benefits by organizations have the potential to impact productivity and presenteeism. For example providing creative spaces, time off to do service work, familial leave for parents to bond with children, or care for elderly/ill loved ones is one such intervention. Exploring the actions and tools that can enable these to occur with minimal disruption to workflow would be worthy of further study. For example devices to remotely monitor loved ones' health or location could be used to diminish concern when not physically present with them, or notify of need for action. Another example could be using sensors that track physiological (heart rate, cortisol release, breathing) signals indicating shifting capacity to handle certain conditions or tasks, resulting in a notification re-assigning the user to a less demanding task, or recommended physical action to counter it (i.e., breathing, walking, sleep).

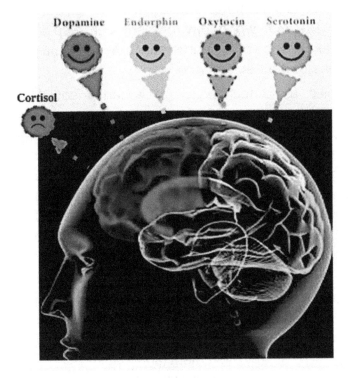

Figure 25. Neurotransmitters stimulated by wellness wearables in this study.

Affordances based on cognitive abilities are challenging to measure when the measurement itself relies on the participants' self-awareness, in this case the indirect effects of an intervention on their sense of presence. Cognitive enhancement as a result of activating the neurotransmitters (see Figure 25) cortisol, serotonin, dopamine, and oxytocin are based on the assumption that the devices used have their intended effect. The devices' functions in the study targeted the issues of physical activity, adequate sleep, mood, focus, posture, and pain management; all of which, if treated, should contribute to better cognitive function (Ratey, 2008; Tavares & Kamimura, 2014; Bergland, 2012; Brennan, 1996; De Beer, 2014). Although the device use may cause the change in behavior or influence the neurotransmitter activity, the effect may be too subtle to capture without sensors monitoring the brain. The real world environment can also influence the perceived experience of the participant, based on the participants' expectations or past experience.

Wearables as a technology to enhance social intelligence (Goleman, 2006; Tan et al., 2012) may not be here yet. This study did not show significant quantifiable increases in presence of mind, one of the attributes of social intelligence. Nonetheless, one must remember that it may be too early to adequately assess, and different tools for measurement might have produced different results. Patience, pause, and reflection prior to reacting, as well as recognizing and avoiding stress triggers were noted by several participants in their interviews. These qualities in interactions are critical for developing trust and conscious business practices (Kofman, 2013).

Context. Personally, my experience with the behavior change as a result of wearables in the fitness/sleep category increased my ability to focus and be my best self at work. Sleep tracking and subtle alarms synched with my movement (and readiness to wake) resulted in better rest: more consistent sleep cycles and increased alertness when awake. Idleness alarms triggered my action to movement increasing blood flow to my brain and body, which refreshed my focus, mood, and energy when I returned to work after a brief pause.

During the course of the study, I tested many devices and observed my own behavior, although informally. I observed the impact of "life happening" regarding my choice of device engagement and human engagement. Seamless integration into my existing tech and lifestyle ecosystem became apparent in well-planned and executed UX design. Being a member of the target demographic provided insight into the challenges and opportunities for this study. As mentioned previously, the interest in wearables as a potential intervention for presence of mind in the workplace was based on my own lived experience.

The Question. The primary research question for this study was "are there affordances from wellness wearable technologies that correlate with sense of presence-of-mind in the workplace?" The mixed-methods approach of the study provided insight into this, but not concrete answers. The presence assessment portion (quantitative) was not conclusive either way. The assessment scores normalized after 7 weeks of wearables use showing neither increased nor decreased presence. The interview responses (qualitative) provided greater definition in the effect on the sense of presence and identification of the affordances from the wearables. One participant remarked, "being alert of slouching and then correcting it helped me maintain my posture most of the working day. I did feel that this allowed me to be more focused in doing the task at hand."

Researching a question often produces more questions than answers. Nonetheless, greater insight is gained in the process. For example, what part of the treatment is the affordance attributed to: the presence assessment, participating in a study on "wearables and presence," or the wearable itself? Was sociomateriality achieved? As one participant stated, "Although it's hard to know if it is related to wearing the device, I seem to have gotten better at detecting stress in my partner and defusing it before it leads to conflict." A longer period of study commencing with only the assessment, followed by wearable use combined with the assessment, would be one way of determining this in a future study. Interviewing in between treatments and at the end would be necessary to capture the participants' awareness of the experience when it is still fresh. To further clarify, an interview done at the start of the study prior to assessments but after they have been notified of qualification into the study, would provide a more accurate identification of the source of the affordance.

Methodologies for research of wearables and presenteeism. This study contributes to understanding of methodologies for research of wearables and presenteeism. The design of this research intended to represent the demographics of a contemporary workforce (culturally, generationally, and gender diverse) and contemporary workplace environment (blend of onsite, offsite, and mixed). This began with the selection criteria for the participants using my extended network (first to third-degree connections) via social media tools (LinkedInTM, FacebookTM, and TwitterTM) and followers of my blog at www.forbesoste.com. By virtue of the format of the invitation/registration (SurveyMonkey.netTM) and devices that all required smart phones, participants had a certain level of tech savvy and comfort with social technologies.

Some devices were upgraded to newer versions from the time of the pilot (3 months prior) and all had upgraded apps. This exemplified the challenge of working with emergent technologies that are rapidly changing. In an effort to provide the authentic user experience and avoid skewing results, participants were provided only standard manufacturer instructions on the devices and apps. They were directed to the manufacturer with all device and use questions. The researcher responded to questions specific to the study. Some participants expressed frustration related to lack of instruction or response to device issues, and others shared their positive experience with the responsiveness of customer service to their issues or questions.

The impact of customer issue response and resolution, particularly in smaller companies without the infrastructure for customer support is worthy of further mention. The rapidly changing landscape lends to an emphasis on the design, manufacturing, distributing, and launching of products. This focus and resource allocation could result in failure to develop sufficient customer support, and device abandonment by users prior to experiencing the benefit of the device.

The assignment of devices was based upon participants' issues (pain management, stress, mood, fitness, sleep, focus) they would like to address, identified in the registration process. The matching process was done manually based on the availability of devices and in some cases the proximity of the participants when sharing a device (in the case of MuseTM, the EEG device). In addition, when possible, participants, known to be peers, were assigned the same device to provide opportunity to take advantage of the social features (such as the UP24TM and Max). Refining the assignment of devices to better align their function with cause of users' presenteeism would be worth exploring in future studies. The degree of presenteeism should also be of consideration; for example, participants' acknowledgement of stifled productivity as a result of a particular issue, rather than selecting an issue they would like to address.

Using the wearable vibrator in a study on presence proved to be both fascinating and challenging. Feedback revealed that some participants were already experiencing regular oxytocin release either with a partner or another non-wearable device. Their motivation for the device selection was more comparative than needs based. In the methodology used, no selection criteria filtered these participants out. As a result, the scores and interviews for participants using these devices might have been skewed. Those who selected it based on need (hormone-related depression) completed the online assessments but most were not comfortable with sharing their experiences in the interviews, despite anonymity. Despite the known benefits of sexual health and release of oxytocin both physically and psychologically, they are a challenge to study as a result of the taboos. Of course, this could be the source of further research opportunities; for example, exploring how to overcome the taboos in order to get accurate research findings related to release of oxytocin as a result of orgasm when using devices in this category. Using a vibrator as one of the wearables invited both curious and critical attention unnecessarily focused away from the study itself in certain audiences.

The automated email invitation used for the weekly survey and reminders had some additional challenges. Managing overflowing inboxes and abundance of notifications can result in unintentional deletion, automatic archive, or oversight by participants. There were frequent requests to re-send the link as well as those who simply did not respond. Despite the recommendation to complete weekly surveys upon receipt, there was variation in when the surveys were actually completed. This was also the case for the primary interviews that were done in the form of an email attachment. The attachment was a pdf form to be completed, saved, and emailed back. Many of them came back empty resulting in lost data. Several responded to the request to resave and resend, but not all. A second effort with the questions embedded in the email text, requiring only reply to the email proved easier for the remaining participants. In addition, there was an increase in more thorough responses. Direct interviews, face-to-face and phone, proved the most rich in content. Direct interviews also provide the opportunity to capture additional information regarding the experience and the users' expectations not in the base questionnaire. Recommendation for future research is that only direct interviews be used for all participants.

Limitations

Data and devices were restricted to those that were available at the starting point of the study (February 2015). Newer versions of some of the devices used in the study just 7 months earlier, have already been released and all smart phone applications are updated and improved (some during the 7 weeks of the study). It is therefore important not to focus on device-specific results, but rather the potential of the category, in the context of this study. Targeting issues that result in presenteeism using wearables is only part of the equation. As the devices improve, so does their potential to factors such as stress, chronic pain, sleep, distraction, fitness, and mood that impact presenteeism. The fact that they are not completely successful yet, is not an indication of their potential, but rather an indication of their lack of maturity.

Doing research in rapidly changing contexts is similar to shooting at a moving target. The devices used in this study were a combination of pre-release and newly released at the time they were distributed in early 2015. At that time, the Human Cloud Studies (Rackspace & Goldsmith, 2013, 2014) and Wilson (2013) studies were among the only previously published works on wearables in the workplace. Because design thinking in organizations and product development are increasingly popular topics for research, there should be more studies in the near future. Similarly, the interest in consciousness in organizations has also seen a sharp increase in popularity. The volume of mainstream articles and issue themes shows the growing widespread interest in design thinking, wearables, and presence (as mindfulness), as seen in Figure 26. In order to complete this study, limited new material was considered from mid-March of 2015 for inclusion.

Figure 26. Design, wearables and
presence in mainstream media

Future Research

Social. Future research should consider the potential for integrating social features and measurement of the quality of interactions. The interviews provided insights into the additional motivating factors of group participation in the study. For example, feedback loops were also desired as to answer the question, "how am I doing?" With the increased interest in mindfulness in organizations, it is worth exploring the measurement process itself as a motivator for mindfulness. In Wilson's (2013) physiolytics, the data becomes the motivator, but it requires the trigger and ability with motivation (Fogg, 2007) for the behavior to change. That said, some participants who were already mindfulness practitioners found the idea of measuring mindfulness or gamifying the exercise counter to the intent. Caution must be exercised when the outcome is overshadowed by the action creating undesirable affordances (i.e., competitive mindfulness). Connection of likeminded and/or motivated users will enable them to experience the social aspects in the context that works best for them. Unless as a mentor, avoid matching a triathlete with someone trying to increase his or her movement to overcome obesity or a seasoned daily mindfulness practitioner with someone who is just learning to take 10 breaths before a stressful action.

Beyond measurement, it would be of great value to explore the entity that is the result of sociomateriality, particularly in the case of emergent technologies' fusion with human and organizational systems. As the devices and consciousness evolve and become more seamlessly integrated, understanding how to best meet the demands and overcome the limitations of the future work-life and digital ecosystems will be critical. Discovering how to avoid treating them as separate entities once they have fused. Exploring failure and success of the fused entity, will help to develop technology and interventions in the future. Looking beyond wearables as devices to their potential role as a means for further integration with the human and organizational system by virtue of their fusion and augmentation through sensors and signals.

Interventions for presenteeism. One potential way to achieve a measurement of presenteeism could be based on changes in productivity in the context of the contemporary workplace; for example, Expanding on the study by De Beer (2014), replace the standing desk with a posture-training wearable for participants with acknowledged back pain during a control period to establish a connection with their output in productivity. This would allow for active measurement that linked the wearable with the measurement-based productivity on a fixed task. This case is less generalizable but could provide some insight as to the possibilities of wearables to impact presenteeism in the workplace. Unfortunately this does not measure presence in the broader sense, but it is a potential starting point that may be used to explore further the actions and tools that can be used to influence the ability to be one's best self at work.

AppleWatch™. Shortly after the study commenced, Apple launched their much-anticipated smartwatch. The AppleWatch™ is one of the first wearables that dove below the tip of the iceberg in terms of wearables development and integration. Although too late to be included in the study, I was able to test and observe both my own use and the response of others when I wore it. I am an Apple person when it comes to devices (each family member has an iPhone™, iPad™, and MacBook Air™). Nonetheless, I tried to be objective. Most notable was the ease with which it integrated into my tech ecosystem and lifestyle. The sociomateriality of my relationship with the device, by virtue of wearing it daily resulted in a comfortable reliance.

Idleness is a consistent struggle, especially when spending long hours in research or writing mode. The hourly haptic notification on my wrist brought my attention to the need to move. This both triggered my posture and movement. Another user working in an organization with wider adoption of the AppleWatch™, shared his observation of group behavior change as a result of the stand alert. The alert, synced at 10 minutes before the hour, was causing meetings to close on time, allowing time for the next meetings (scheduled to start at the top of the hour) to start on time. This behavior triggered even non-watch wearers who, observing the watch wearers standing as a cue, became aware that it was a 10-minute warning to wrap up the meeting. Because co-workers knew about the device as the trigger, the act of standing was recognized as a wellness behavior, rather than an impolite non-verbal cue of impatience.

One of the more subtle features of the device with the potential to influence presence is a mute function. Covering the face of the AppleWatch™ mutes the sound and turns off the screen. This action and consequential result is useful when watching a movie, but also in conversation with others. The action of covering the face then becomes a non-verbal cue by the users that they intend to be present with the person or people with whom they are interacting.

As a social cue, the watch was often a status symbol early after its launch. Living in the Bay Area where digital citizens are the norm at all ages, this symbolism was less apparent. When traveling in other regions it became more of a conversation piece. I was often stopped to ask what I thought of it, or volunteered a story from a fellow AppleWatch™ user. At a wearables event, I was caught in a heated discussion with a timepiece journalist about smartwatch solutions for designer watches versus smartwatches. The difference between a mobile phone and a smartphone raised similar debates in 2007 at the launch of the iPhoneTM. Over 70% of the U.S. population now has a smart phone (Pew Research Center, 2015). The AppleWatch™ was a statement piece while it was still new and elicited varying (positive, negative, and neutral) non-verbal responses.

Since its launch in March, several competitors have launched similar products that extend the category of smartwatches. The Gear2TM used in the study was an early example of this. There are many more features to the newer generation of devices beyond fitness/health tracking, timekeeping, communications, and notifications. In particular, they provide an alternate interface for many of the other wearables in addition to collecting data that contribute to health apps. Future research with smartwatches will provide insight into where they fit in terms of influence on presence.

Conclusion

The potential for wearables to achieve sociomateriality fusing the human and organization with technology is inherent in their personal form. Wearables today are still very much in their infancy. Despite the rapid growth and adoption in developed markets, the devices are still in a rudimentary form. Nevertheless, willingness of consumers to experiment with the devices has boosted the growth of the market. Design elements in the form of power, connection, form factor, and even function currently limit the potential for fully seamless integration into the already complex lives of the users.

The contemporary workplace is not a controlled environment. This study was representative of the real world conditions and variables. It was not intended to provide statistically significant results that did not "depend" on context of covariates. A controlled study would most likely have such a great effect on the results that the study would not be valid for real world application. Further quantitative and qualitative measures could be added in order to get a more accurate account for change in presence by providing 360° feedback-using peers. Additional assessments should be reviewed for further validity in this case.

Wearables still have a way to go as far as improving accuracy, cost, and design before their recognized added value outweighs their perceived risks to diminished presence. Increased awareness of benefit to collecting personal data will eventually outweigh fear of the next generation of wearables, embeddables. Whether ingestible (by mouth), injectable (into system), or implanted (under skin) the form factor will have to be justified by the value its level of invasiveness permits (preventative health and wellness, safety, enhanced capabilities). In this study, as well as in the Human Cloud Study (Rackspace & Goldsmith, 2013), there was less concern over privacy than anticipated. The convenience of passive data collection, seamless integration, and human power generation for the devices will be critical. Context is vital to avoid contributing to presenteeism rather than countering it.

Wearables and wellness as a challenge to productivity in organizations has received much press at the time of this study in 2015. These findings did not confirm the wearables used in the study as a solution to hindered presence, but neither were they confirmed as the source. The concern for the wearables to be the source of presenteeism was unfounded in the case of this study. This study showed no significant change as a result of wearables use while completing a presence assessment weekly. Continued studies as the technology evolves will be needed. The improvements in the latest or next generation of wearables or embeddables could provide different results.

Mid-career professionals have many interruptions that hinder consistent adoption of new technologies, even if recognized as beneficial. Approaching the challenges associated with taking the anomaly as the norm, bring your own device (BYOD) programs will generate better context and results. Recognizing the complexities of human factors, the context of the contemporary workplace and workforce, their tech ecosystem and the general ecosystem in which work takes place requires systems thinking and innovation in order to come up with effective solutions.

User interface design (UX design) is increasingly important for solutions that deal with the complexities of the various forms of presenteeism. One use may be to assist in preventative health and wellness initiatives. This seamless integration will require collaboration and shared standards for developing platform-agnostic devices that provide relevant data in formats that can be used for preventative health by providers and by the users themselves. Emphasis on UX design will contribute to better solutions that deal with the complexities of the various forms of presenteeism.

Identifying tools to enhance the ability to be present and aware requires recognizing the complexity of the human condition and its dynamic environment. As such, there is no simple quick fix. Bringing one's attention to the need for presence is a primary first step. It is critical to identify the root causes of presenteeism and matching them with effective tools to treat the context and relevant conditions. The broader definition of presenteeism, including health-related, disengagement, and conscious presenteeism, should be applied to treating these conditions. The contemporary workplace and workforce require a multifaceted approach to countering the physiological and psychological conditions that hinder the ability to be present. Productivity measures, self-assessment, and feedback from others should be included in measurement of the effectiveness of the treatment. Self-assessment alone will not provide accurate data on presence.

Being one's best self at work requires both presence and action, as does bringing out the best in others. Advances in this emerging category of technology have the potential to impact both, but they are not there yet. With continued efforts to achieve sociomateriality between the devices and the human and organizational systems, there is great potential in understanding what tools and actions enable the best result.

References

ABI Research. (2013). Wearable Computing Device Shipments by Type, World Market, Forecast: 2013 to 2020. Wearable Device Market Share and Forecasts. Retrieved from https://www.abiresearch.com/market-research/product/1019580-wearable-device-market-share-and-forecasts/

Archer, D. (2013, July 25). Smartphone addiction. Psychology Today [blog post]. Retrieved from http://www.psychologytoday.com/blog/reading-between-the-headlines/201307/

smartphone-addiction

Bartz, J. A., Zaki, J., Bolger, N., Hollander, E., Ludwig, N. N., Kolevzon, A., & Ochsner, K. N. (2010). Oxytocin selectively improves empathic accuracy. Psychological Science, 21(10), 1426-1428. doi: 10.1177/0956797610383439

Beeli, G., Casutt, G., Baumgartner, T., & Jancke, L. (2008). Modulating presence and impulsiveness by external stimulation of the brain. Behavioral and Brain Functions, 4(1), 33.

Bergland, C. (2012). The neurochemicals of happiness. The athlete's way. Psychology Today [blog post] Retrieved from http://www.psychologytoday.com/blog/the-athletes-way/201211/the-neurochemicals-happiness

Bingham, T., & Conner, M. (2010). The new social learning: A guide to transforming organizations through social media. San Francisco, CA: Berrett-Koehler.

Bingham, T., & Conner, M. (2015). The new social learning: Connect. Collaborate. Work. (2nd ed.). Alexandria, VA: ATD Press.

Birnbaum, H. G., Kessler, R. C., Kelley, D., Ben-Hamadi, R., Joish, V. N., & Greenberg, P. E. (2010). Employer burden of mild, moderate, and severe major depressive disorder: mental health services utilization and costs, and work performance. Depression and Anxiety, 27(1), 78-89. doi:10.1002/da.20580

Brennan, R. (1996). The Alexander technique manual: A step-by-step guide to improve breathing, posture and well-being. Boston, MA: Journey Editions.

Bragazzi, N. L., & Del Puente, G. (2014). A proposal for including nomophobia in the new DSM-V. Psychology Research and Behavior Management, 7, 155-160. doi: 10.2147/PRBM.S41386

Brown, K. W., & Ryan, R. M. (2003). The benefits of being present: Mindfulness and its role in psychological well-being. Journal of Personality and Social Psychology, 84(4), 822-848. doi: 10.1037/0022-3514.84.4.822

Buck Consultants. (2009). Working well: A global survey of health promotion and workplace wellness strategies. Retrieved from http://www.worldatwork.org/waw/adimLink?id=36309

Buck Consultants. (2012). Working well: A global survey of health promotion and workplace wellness strategies. Retrieved from http://www.buckconsultants.com/portals/0/events/2012/web/wa-working-well-what-next-wellness-2012-1212.pdf

Buck Consultants. (2014). Working well: A global survey of health promotion, workplace wellness, and productivity strategies. 6th ed. Retrieved from https://www.bucksurveys.com/BuckSurveys/Portals/0/aspdnsf/BuckSurveys_OrdersDownload/Health%20and%20Productivity/GW_Exec_Summary_Global.pdf

Cancelliere, C., Cassidy, J. D., Ammendolia, C., Côté, P., (2011). Are workplace health promotion programs effective at improving presenteeism in workers? a systematic review and best evidence synthesis of the literature. BMC Public Health. 11:395. http://www.biomedcentral.com/1471-2458/11/395

Carr, L. J., Leonhard, C., Tucker, S., Fethke, N., Benzo, R., & Gerr, F. (2015). Total worker health intervention increases activity of sedentary workers. American Journal of Preventive Medicine. http://dx.doi.org/10.1016/j.amepre.2015.06.022

Centers [KM1] for Disease Control and Prevention. (2014). Insufficient sleep is a public health epidemic. [blogpost] Retrieved from http://www.cdc.gov/features/dssleep/

Chapman, L. (2005). Presenteeism and its role in worksite health promotion. American Journal of Health Promotion, 19(4), 1-8.

Cohen, S., & Janicki-Deverts, D. (2009). Can we improve our physical health by altering our social networks? Perspectives on Psychological Science, 4(4), 375-378. doi: 10.1111/j.1745-6924.2009.01141.x

Cooper, C., & Dewe, P. (2008). Well-being - absenteeism, presenteeism, costs and challenges. Occupational Medicine, 58(8), 522-524. doi: 10.1093/occmed/kqn124

Cuddy, A. J. C., Wilmuth, C. A., & Carney, D. R. (2012). The benefit of power posing before a high-Stakes social evaluation. (Harvard Business School Working Paper No. 13-027). Retrieved from https://dash.harvard.edu/bitstream/handle/1/9547823/13-027.pdf?sequence=1

D'Abate, C. P., & Eddy, E. R. (2007). Engaging in personal business on the job: Extending the presenteeism construct. Human Resource Development Quarterly, 18(3), 361-383. doi: 10.1002/hrdq.1209

Danoff, R. (2015) American Osteopathic Association. Retrieved from http://www.osteopathic.org/osteopathic-health/about-your-health/health-conditions-library/general-health/Pages/chronic-pain.aspx

Dalai Lama (2008). Worlds in harmony: Compassionate action for a better world (2nd ed.). Berkeley, CA: Parallax Press.

De Beer, L. T. (2014). The effect of presenteeism-related health conditions on employee work engagement levels: A comparison between groups. South African Journal of Human Resource

Management / SA Tydskrif vir Menslikehulpbronbestuur, 12(1), 8. doi: http://dx.doi.org/10.4102/sajhrm.v12i1.640

Ding, W., & Lin, X. (2009). Information architecture: The design and integration of information spaces. Synthesis Lectures on Information Concepts, Retrieval, and Services. doi:10.2200/S00214ED1V01Y200910ICR008)

Dishman, L. (2015) These are the top jobs for college graduates in 2015. Fast Company. Retrieved from http://www.fastcompany.com/3047722/the-future-of-work/these-are-the-top-jobs-for-college-graduates-in-2015

Eddy, E. R., D'Abate, C. P., & Thurston, P. W., Jr. (2010). Explaining engagement in personal activities on company time. Personnel Review, 39(5), 639-654. Retrieved from http://dx.doi.org/10.1108/00483481011064181

Edwards, J., Jones, A. D., & Cunningham, T. (2014, November). Effects of mobile phone use on anxiety, depedency, and sleep in medical and health professions graduate level students. Paper presented at the 142nd APHA Annual Meeting and Exposition, New Orleans, LA.

Ehrlich, P. R. (2000). Human natures: Genes, cultures, and the human prospect. New York, NY: Penguin.

Erlich, A., Bichard, J.A., & Myerson, J. (2010). New demographics new workspace. Burlington, VT: Ashgate.

Fagan, M. H. (2014). Exploring a sociomaterial perspective on technology in virtual human resource development. Advances in Developing Human Resources, 16(3), 320-334. doi:10.1177/1523422314532094

Fogg, B. (2003). Persuasive technology: Using computers to change what we think and do. San Francisco, CA: Morgan Kaufman.

Fogg, B. J. (2007). The Fogg behavior model. Retrieved from http://www-personal.umich.edu/~mrother/KATA_Files/FBM.pdf

Forbes Öste, H. (2009). Social optimization. [PowerPoint slides]. Retrieved from http://www.slideshare.net/hcfoste/social-optimization

Forbes Öste, H. (2013). Social optimization theory defined. The Art of Social Strategy. [blog]. Retrieved from http://forbesoste.com/research/social-optimization-theory/files/49/social-optimization-theory.html

Friedman, H. H., & Friedman, L. W. (2015). Taking care of business: Critical leadership ideas. SSRN Electronic Journal, 21. doi:http://dx.doi.org/10.2139/ssrn.2568452

Fry, R. (2015). This year, Millennials will overtake Baby Boomers. Pew Research: Fact Tank: News in Numbers. Retrieved from http://www.pewresearch.org/fact-tank/2015/01/16/this-year-millennials-will-overtake-baby-boomers/

Gates, N., & Valenzuela, M. (2010). Cognitive Exercise and Its Role in Cognitive Function in Older Adults. Current Psychiatry Reports, 12(1), 20-27. doi:10.1007/s11920-009-0085-y

Gaskin, J., Berente, N., Lyytinen, K., & Yoo, Y. (2014). Toward generalizable sociomaterial inquiry: a computational approach for zooming in and out of sociomaterial routines. Mis Quarterly, 38(3), 849-871.

Gaver, W. W. (1996). Situating action II: Affordances for interaction: The social is material for design. Ecological Psychology, 8(2), 111-129.

George, B., Sims, P., & Gergen, D. (2010). True North: Discover Your Authentic Leadership: Wiley.

Gibson, J. J. (1979). The ecological approach to visual perception. Dallas, TX: Houghton Mifflin

Gibson, J. J. (2015). The ecological approach to visual perception: Classic edition. New York, NY: Psychology Press.

Goetzel, R. Z., Long, S. R., Ozminkowski, R. J., Hawkins, K., Wang, S., & Lynch, W. (2004). Health, absence, disability, and presenteeism cost estimates of certain physical and mental health conditions affecting U.S. employers. Journal of Occupational and Environmental Medicine, 46(4), 398-412. Retrieved from http://journals.lww.com/joem/Fulltext/2004/04000/Health,_Absence,_Disability,_and_Presenteeism_Cost.13.aspx

Goleman, D. (2006). Social intelligence. New York, NY: Bantam Dell.

Gummesson, E. (2004). Return on relationships (ROR): the value of relationship marketing and CRM in business to business contexts. Journal of Business & Industrial Marketing, 19(2), 136-148. doi:10.1108/08858620410524016

Hemp, P. (2004). Presenteeism: At work—but out of it. Harvard Business Review, 82, 9.

Hewlett, S. A., Leader-Chivée, L., Sherbin, L., Gordon, J., & Dieudonné, F. (2014). Executive presence. New York, NY: Harper Business.

Hinton, A. (2015). Understanding context environment, language and information architecture. M. Treseler & S. St. Laurent, Eds. [electronic book]. Sebastopol, CA: O'Reilly Media.

Höfling, V., Moosbrugger, H., Schermelleh-Engel, K., & Heidenreich, T. (2011). Mindfulness or mindlessness?: A modified version of the Mindful Attention and Awareness Scale (MAAS). European Journal of Psychological Assessment, 27(1), 59-64. doi: http://dx.doi.org.fgul.idm.oclc.org/10.1027/1015-5759/a000045

Hoshi, K. (2012). Here and now: Foundations and practice of human-experiential design (Doctoral dissertation). Umeå universitet. Retrieved from DIVA: Digitalal Vetenskapliga Arkivet. (diva2:514982)

Huffington, A. (2014). Thrive: The Third Metric to Redefining Success and Creating a Life of Well-being, Wisdom, and Wonder: Random House LLC.

International HapMap 3 Consortium (2010). Integrating common and rare genetic variation in diverse human populations. Nature, 467, 52-8. doi:10.1038/nature09298

Jhansi, R. & Krishna, R. (1996). Meditation and attention regulation, Journal of Indian Psychology, 14(1-2), 26-30.

Kabat-Zinn, J. (2007). Full catastrophe living: Using the wisdom of your body and mind to face stress, pain, and illness [Audible edition]. New York, NY: Random House.

Kahn, W. A. (1992). To be fully there: Psychological presence at work. Human Relations, 45(4), 321.

Kärkkäinen, H., Jussila, J., & Väisänen, J. (2010). Social media use and potential in business-to-business companies' innovation. Paper presented at the 14th International Academic MindTrek Conference: Envisioning Future Media Environments, Tampere, Finland.

Kofman, F. (2013). Conscious business:How to build value through values. Louisville, CO: Sounds True.

Komisaruk, B. R., Beyer-Flores, C., & Whipple, B. (2006) Science of orgasm. Baltimore, MD: Johns Hopkins University Press.

Kukekov, V. G., Laywell, E. D., Suslov, O., Davies, K., Scheffler, B., Thomas, L. B.,... Steindler, D. A. (1999). Multipotent stem/progenitor cells with similar properties arise from two neurogenic regions of adult human brain. Experimental Neurology, 156(2), 333-344. doi: 10.1006/exnr.1999.7028

Lake, D. A. (2011). Why "isms" are evil: Theory, epistemology, and academic sects as impediments to understanding and progress. International Studies Quarterly, 55(2), 465-480. doi: 10.1111/j.1468-2478.2011.00661.x

Langer, E., Chanowitz, B., & Blank, A. (1985). Mindlessness–mindfulness in perspective: A reply to Valerie Folkes. Journal of Personality and Social Psychology, 48(3), 605-607. doi:10.1037/0022-3514.48.3.605

Langer, E. J. (1989). Mindful matters: The consequences of mindlessness - mindfulness. In L. Berkowitz (Ed.), Advances in experimental psychology. (pp. 137-173). New York, NY: Academic Press, Inc.

Langer, E. J. (2009). Counterclockwise: Mindful health and the power of possibility. New York, NY: Random House.

Langer, E. J. (2014). Mindfulness (25th anniversary ed.). Boston, MA: Da Capo Press.

Langley, P., Müller-Schwefe, G., Nicolaou, A., Liedgens, H., Pergolizzi, J., & Varrassi, G. (2010). The impact of pain on labor force participation, absenteeism and presenteeism in the European Union. Journal of Medical Economics, 13(4), 662-672.

Landsberger, H. A. (1958). Hawthorne revisited: Management and the worker, its critics, and developments in human relations in industry (Vol. 9). Ithaca, NY: Cornell University.

Leonardi, P. M. (2013). Theoretical foundations for the study of sociomateriality. Information and Organization, 23(2), 59-76. doi:http://dx.doi.org/10.1016/j.infoandorg.2013.02.002

Li, C. (2010). Open leadership: How social technology can transform the way you lead. Hoboken, NJ: John Wiley & Sons.

Li, C., & Solis, B. (2013). The seven success factors of social business strategy. San Francisco, CA: Jossey-Bass.

Mayo Clinic (2015) Stress symptoms: Effects on your body and behavior (Healthy Lifestyle). Retrieved from http://www.mayoclinic.org/healthy-lifestyle/stress-management/in-depth/stress-symptoms/art-20050987

McEwen, B. S., & Stellar, E. (1993). Stress and the individual: Mechanisms leading to disease. Archives of Internal Medicine, 153(18), 2093-2101. doi:10.1001/archinte.1993.00410180039004

Merchant, N. (2012). 11 rules for creating value in the social era. Cambridge, MA: Harvard Business Review Press.

Meeker, M., & Wu, L. (2013). Internet Trends D11 Conference. Kleiner Perkins Caulfield Byers. Retrieved from http://www.slideshare.net/kleinerperkins/kpcb-internet-trends-2013

Mishra, G., & Evans, D. (Producers). (2009). 20:20 Social Position Paper on Social Business Strategy. Retrieved from http://www.

slideshare.net/2020social/2020social-position-paper-social-business-strategy-september-2009

Mobile 50. (2007). Facts about the mobile. A journey through time: The 50th anniversary of the mobile phone. Retrieved from http://web.archive.org/web/20100813122017/http://

www.mobilen50ar.se/eng/FaktabladENGFinal.pdf

Moggridge, B. (2007). Designing interactions. Cambridge: Massachusetts Institute of Technology Press.

Molm, L. D. (2010). The Structure of Reciprocity. Social Psychology Quarterly, 73(2), 119-131. Retrieved from https://fgul.idm.oclc.org/login?url=http://search.proquest.com/docview/907550799?accountid=10868

Morgan, W. D., & Morgan, S. T. (2005). Cultivating attention and empathy. In C.K. Germer, R.D. Siegel, & P.R. Fulton (Eds.), Mindfulness and psychotherapy (pp. 73-90). New York, NY: Guilford Publications.

Motti, V. G., & Caine, K. (2014). Human factors considerations in the design of wearable devices. Proceedings of the Human Factors and Ergonomics Society Annual Meeting, 58(1), 205-209. doi:10.1177/1541931214581381

Mutch, A. (2013). Sociomateriality — A wrong turning? Information and Organization, 23(1), 28–40. http://dx.doi.org/10.1016/j.infoandorg.2013.02.001

Myers, K. A. (2011). Metanoia and the transformation of opportunity. Rhetoric Society Quarterly, 41(1), 1-18. doi: 10.1080/02773945.2010.533146

National Sleep Foundation. (2008). 2008 Sleep in America poll: Summary of findings. Retrieved from https://sleepfoundation.org/media-center/press-release/sleep-america-poll-summary-findings

Nevejan, C., & Gill, S. P. (2012). Witnessed presence. AI & Society, 27(1), 1-4. doi: http://dx.doi.org.fgul.idm.oclc.org/10.1007/s00146-011-0363-1

Nielson (2014). Mobile millennials: Over 85% of Generation Y owns smartphones: Mobile. Retrieved from http://www.nielsen.com/us/en/insights/news/2014/mobile-millennials-over-85-percent-of-generation-y-owns-smartphones.html

Nirmala. (2015). What is spiritual enlightenment or spiritual awakening?. Retrieved from http://endless-satsang.com/spiritual-enlightenment-spiritual-awakening.htm

Norman, D. A. (1988). The Psychology of Everyday Things: New York, NY: Basic Books.

Norman, D. (1999). Affordances, conventions and design. Interactions, 6(3), 38-43. doi: 10.1145/301153.301168

Norman, D. (2009). The design of future things. New York, NY: Basic books.

Norman, D. (2013). The design of everyday things: Revised and expanded edition: Basic books.

Nowak, M. A., & Sigmund, K. (2000). Shrewd investments. Science, 288(5467), 819-820. doi:10.1126/science.288.5467.819

Orlikowski, W.J. 2007. Sociomaterial practices: Exploring technology at work. Organization Studies, 28: 1435–1448

Orlikowski, W. J., & Scott, S. V. (2008). 10   Sociomateriality: Challenging the separation of technology, work and organization. The Academy of Management Annals, 2(1), 433-474. doi:10.1080/19416520802211644

Owen, N., Healy, G. N., Matthews, C. E., & Dunstan, D. W. (2010). Too much sitting: The population-health science of sedentary behavior. Exercise and Sport Sciences Reviews, 38(3), 105–113. http://doi.org/10.1097/JES.0b013e3181e373a2

Parmiggiani, E., & Mikalsen, M. (2013). The facets of sociomateriality: A systematic mapping of emerging concepts and definitions. In M. Aanestad & T. Bratteteig (Eds.), Nordic Contributions in IS Research (Vol. 156, pp. 87-103): Springer Berlin Heidelberg.

Patel, B. (2015). Mobile medical applications: Guidance for the industry and Food and Drug Administration staff. Retrieved from http://www.fda.gov/downloads/MedicalDevices/ DeviceRegulationandGuidance/GuidanceDocuments/ UCM263366.pdf

Pew Research Center. (2015) The smartphone difference: U.S smartphone use in 2015. Numbers, Facts and Trends Shaping the World. Retrieved from http://www.pewinternet. org/2015/04/01/us-smartphone-use-in-2015/

Pirson, M. A., Langer, E., Bodner, T. E., & Zilcha-Mano, S. (2012). The development and validation of the Langer Mindfulness Scale - Enabling a socio-cognitive perspective of mindfulness in organizational contexts. SSRN Electronic Journal, 54. doi:10.2139/ssrn.2158921

Rackspace & Institute of Management Studies at Goldsmiths, University London. (2013). The human cloud at work: Wearable technology from novelty to productivity. London, England. Retrieved from http://www.rackspace.co.uk/sites/default/files/ whitepapers/The_Human_Cloud_-_June_2013.pdf

Rackspace & Institute of Management Studies at Goldsmiths, University London. (2014). The human cloud at work: A study into the impact of wearable technologies in the workplace. London, England. Retrieved from https://www.rackspace.co.uk/ sites/default/files/Human%20Cloud%20at%20Work.pdf

Ratey, J. J. (2008). Spark: The revolutionary new science of exercise and the brain. New York, NY: Little, Brown.

Reid, D. (2008). Exploring the relationship between occupational presence, occupational engagement, and people's well being. Journal of Occupational Science, 15(1), 43-47. doi: 10.1080/14427591.2008.9686606

Reid, D. (2009). Capturing presence moments: The art of mindful practice in occupational therapy. The Canadian Journal of Occupational Therapy, 76(3), 180-188.

Rheingold & Weeks. (2012). Net smart: How to thrive online. Cambridge, MA: MIT Press

Richardson, J. R. & Gwaltney, W. A. (2005). Ship it!: A practical guide to successful software projects. Raleigh, NC: Pragmatic Bookshelf.

Riva, G. (2008, October). Presence and social presence: From agency to self and others. Paper presented at the 11th Annual International Workshop on Presence, Padova, Italy.

Riva, G., Waterworth, J. A., & Waterworth, E. L. (2004). The layers of presence: A bio-cultural approach to understanding presence in natural and mediated environments. CyberPsychology & Behavior, 7(4), 402-416. doi: 10.1089/cpb.2004.7.402

Robertson, I. H. (2000). Mind sculpture: Your brain's untapped potential. New York, NY: Fromm International.

Rosekind, M. R., Gregory, K. B., Mallis, M. M., Brandt, S. L., Seal, B., & Lerner, D. (2010). The cost of poor sleep: workplace productivity loss and associated costs. Journal of Occupational and Environmental Medicine, 52(1), 91-98.

Rowland, C., Goodman, E., Charlier, M., Light, A., & Lui, A. (2015). Designing connected products: UX for the consumer internet of things (1st ed.). Sebastopol, CA: O'Reilly Media.

Rubin, T. (2014). How to look people in the eye digitally San Jose, CA: Substantium.

Saltonstall, R. (1959). Human relations in administration, text and cases. New York, NY: McGraw-Hill.

Scharmer, C. O. (2000, March). Presencing: Learning from the future as it emerges. Paper presented at the Conference on Knowledge and Innovation, Helsinki, Finland.

Scharmer, C. O. (2009). Theory U: Learning from the future as it emerges: Berrett-Koehler Publishers.

Scheflen, A. E. (1964). The significance of posture in communication systems. Psychiatry, 27(4), 316-331.

Schein, C. (2014). The value of integrating social media tools into organizational learning processes. (doctoral dissertation), Fielding Graduate University, ProQuest Dissertations Publishing. (3611907)

Senge, P. M., Scharmer, C. O., Jaworski, J., & Flowers, B. S. (2005). Presence: An exploration of profound change in people, organizations, and society. New York, NY: Crown.

Siegel, D. J. (2007). The mindful brain: Reflection and attunement in the cultivation of well-being (Norton Series on Interpersonal Neurobiology. New York, NY: WW Norton.

Solis, B. (2015). X: The experience when business meets design. Hoboken, NJ: John Wiley & Sons.

Tan, C. M., Goleman, D., & Kabat-Zinn, J. (2014). Search inside yourself: The unexpected path to achieving success, happiness (and world peace). New York, NY: HarperCollins.

Tavares, R. d. S. C. R., & Kamimura, Q. P. (2014). Productivity and presenteeism - A question of sleeping well. Independent Journal of Management & Production, 5(2), 417-437.

TechSci Research. (2015). Global Smart Wearables Market Forecast and Opportunities, 2020. Retrieved from http://www.techsciresearch.com/report/global-smart-wearables-market-forecast-and-opportunities-2020/435.html

Thierer, A. (2014) The internet of things and wearable technology: Addressing privacy and security concerns without derailing innovation. Richmond Journal of Law and Technology, 21(6), 118. Retrieved from http://dx.doi.org/10.2139/ssrn.2494382

Turgiss, J., Allen, S., & Xiao, S. (2015). Asleep on the Job: The Causes and Consequences of Employees' Disrupted Sleep and How Employers Can Help. Retrieved from http://connect.virginpulse.com/asleep-on-the-job-report-from-virgin-pulse.pdf

Turkle, S. (2011). Alone together: Why we expect more from technology and less from each other. New York, NY: Basic Books.

U.S. Department of Health and Human Services, Food and Drug Administration, Center for Devices and Radiological Health. (2015). General Wellness: Policy for Low Risk Devices; Draft Guidance for Industry and Food and Drug Administration Staff. Retrieved from http://www.fda.gov/downloads/MedicalDevices/ DeviceRegulationandGuidance/GuidanceDocuments/ UCM429674.pdf

Waterworth, J., & Riva, G. (2014). Feeling present in the physical world and in computer mediated environments. London, England: Palgrave Pivot.

Wendel, S. (2014). Designing for behavior change: Applying psychology and behavioral economics. Sebastopol, CA: O'Reilly Media.

Wilson, H. J. (2013, September). Wearables in the workplace. Harvard Business Review. Retrieved from https://hbr. org/2013/09/wearables-in-the-workplace

World Health Organization (WHO). Constitution entered into force on 7 April 1948 (Preamble)

Wurman, R.S. (1996). Information architects. (n.p.). Graphis Press Corp.

Yamasue, H., Yee, J. R., Hurlemann, R., Rilling, J. K., Chen, F. S., Meyer-Lindenberg, A., & Tost, H. (2012). Integrative approaches utilizing oxytocin to enhance prosocial behavior: From animal and human social behavior to autistic social dysfunction. The Journal of Neuroscience, 32(41), 14109-14117a. doi:10.1523/ jneurosci.3327-12.2012

This dissertation edition formatting is slightly modified to accommodate reading in an ebook or book format. This version was created at the request of individuals who do not have access to the scholars databases. The content has not been modified other than removal of appendices required for submission.

Can I Ask You For A Favor?

If you'd like to leave a review then please visit the link below:

http://bit.ly/2gsZqKf

If you are interested in how this work is being applied in practice, follow me on Facebook https://www.facebook.com/DrForbesOste/

Or check out the Digital Self Mastery™ movement on Facebook

https://www.facebook.com/groups/DigitalSelfMastery

Digital Self Mastery is the work that brings the BE-ing@ Work research and the behavior science behind our relationship with technology into the language and perspective of the greater community and the book that brings sociomateriality into practice.

Digital Self Mastery http://bit.ly/2xq4Tfa

Thanks for your support!

About The Author

Dr. Heidi Forbes Öste is a behavioral scientist passionate about the potential for technology and wellbeing innovations to enhance the ability to be one's best. She combines 25 years experience in social technologies and social strategy for organizations with research in presence-of-mind, wellbeing technology, and the user experience. A scholar, practitioner, connector and global citizen.

Her motto: Knowledge is Power, Sharing is Powerful.

Find out more at http://2BalanceU.com

http://bit.ly/2gsZqKf

www.ingramcontent.com/pod-product-compliance
Lightning Source LLC
LaVergne TN
LVHW092010050326
832904LV00002B/41